A Shared Destiny

Indu Capoor is Founder-Director of Centre for Health, Education, Training and Nutrition Awareness (CHETNA), based in Ahmedabad, Gujarat, India, an organisation she started when she was just 23 years old. Trained as a nutritionist, she has spent over three decades working with women, children and young people, particularly those from marginalised communities, to improve their health and nutritional status. In 2013, Indu passed on leadership of CHETNA and took on the role of Director, CHETNA Outreach, to upscale and mainstream CHETNA's evidence based approaches all over the globe.

Widely travelled, Indu is the recipient of several national and international awards, has, extensively published and spoken about effects of gender and social determinants on maternal, young people's, child health and rights in nearly 2,500 workshops, seminars and conferences. She was elected as an ASHOKA Associate Member in 1992 and a Global Leader on Early Childhood Care and Development (ECCD) in 2009.

INDU CAPOOR

A Shared Destiny

My Journey with CHETNA

ACADEMIC FOUNDATION
NEW DELHI

www.academicfoundation.org

First published in 2017 *by*

ACADEMIC FOUNDATION

Delhi Sales Office:
4772-73 / 23 Bharat Ram Road,
(23 Ansari Road), Darya Ganj,
New Delhi - 110 002 (India).
Phones : 23245001 / 02 / 03 / 04.
Fax : +91-11-23245005.

Corporate Office:
No. 35, Sector 7,
IMT Manesar,
Gurgaon - 122050.
Haryana (India).
Tel: +91-124-4215070 / 71.

E-mail : books@academicfoundation.com
www.academicfoundation.org

Disclaimer:
The findings/views/opinions expressed in this book are solely those of the author and do not necessarily reflect the views of the publisher.

Cataloging in Publication Data--DK
Courtesy: D.K. Agencies (P) Ltd. <docinfo@dkagencies.com>

Capoor, Indu, author.
A shared destiny : my journey with CHETNA / Indu Capoor.
pages cm
ISBN 9789332703780

1. Capoor, Indu. 2. Centre for Health Education, Training and Nutrition Awareness (Ahmadābād, India)--Biography. 3. Centre for Health Education, Training and Nutrition Awareness (Ahmadābād, India)--History. 4. Non-governmental organizations--India. 5. Sex role in the work environment--India. 6. Women in community organization--India. I. Title.

HV394.I43C46 2016 DDC 361.763095475 23

Printed and bound by The Book Mint, New Delhi.
www.thebookmint.in

Praise for the Book

(Continue from the back cover)

A fascinating account of personal and institutional growth in a sector on which so much of human well being depends.

— **Shri Ashoke Chatterjee,** Board of Trustee, Prabhat Education Foundation, Ahmedabad; Former Executive Director, National Institute of Design (NID), Ahmedabad

Indu Capoor's book opens a window to the fascinating but changing world of gender discrimination, realities of the health of women and children in India's hinterland, challenges in the social sector space and more importantly, how an organisation like CHETNA can whip up change and hope.

— **Ramesh Menon,** author, film maker and editor.

Indu Capoor's book is a highly readable story of personal and organisational evolution. Born from a lifelong dedication to the ideals of gender equality and wholesome leadership, Indu's narrative is both informative and compelling. This book is a must read for all those who care for co-creating more equitable organisations and evolving a society more caring towards women and the environment.

— **Arun Wakhlu,** Executive Chairman, Pragati Leadership Institute, Pune; Former Governing Council Member, CHETNA (2006-2013)

A fascinating account of the criss-cross of personal and professional challenges in the complex journey of women centred institution building.

— **Dr. Sharada Jain,** Founder and Director Sandhan Society, Jaipur; Founding Chairperson of Governance Board, CHETNA (2002-2014)

Civil society founder-leaders rarely reflect on their organisation-building experiences in India, or around the world. Even rare is the gender lens for understanding social change organisations. From both these perspectives, Indu's story of CHETNA is remarkably and provocatively told. From young civil society leaders to students of organisation-building, a range of readers would find this book gripping.

— **Dr. Rajesh Tandon,** Founding Member and President, Participatory Research in Asia (PRIA), New Delhi; Co-Chair, UNESCO (Community Based Research and Social Responsibility in Higher Education)

Contents

Section THREE

Building a Gender Sensitive Organisation

Section FOUR

Re-visioning Organisations

Foreword

Till the mid 70s, the Nehru Foundation Development (NFD) operationalised its work through one institution, the Vikram A. Sarabhai Community Science Centre (VASCSC). At that time, we had started work on the new campus at Thaltej on the outskirts of Ahmedabad. There was much discussion as to what should be the core philosophy of NFD. Dr Vikram Sarabhai had written two paragraphs, which were critical to these discussions:

> The Foundation.....would provide the forum and the staff services to support the initiative of individuals who are interested in similar problems of development. Through the proposed Foundation, we would attempt to create intellectual resource groups supported by those who feel motivated to think and to share their thinking with others on problems of current interest. The Foundation would explore ideas and communicate, but it would not concern itself directly with implementation.

> Operationally, the Foundation would identify individuals who are interested in its activities and can contribute to its objectives. Locally they would be able to interact on a continuing basis, using the Foundation as a focal point. From outside Ahmedabad, they would be invited and encouraged to spend time from a few days to some months if they can. They would produce papers for study and serious discussions.

The Vikram Sarabhai Centre for Development Interaction (VIKSAT) was established in 1976 to work on issues addressing development in general and later focusing on social issues of Ahmedabad. A survey was conducted inquiring what the essential characteristics of the city should be in the year 2000, a distant vision at that time. One of the important responses that was received was related to the safety of women and the fact that women should feel comfortable and safe travelling at night. This was the first word used in the context of social environment.

As VIKSAT grew, issues relating to governance and institutional building became extremely important. We felt that the NFD could support social entrepreneurs and build institutions around them. At VIKSAT, a small core team was gathering, both people who were driven by passion and those seeking a job.

In the early 1980s, the forerunner to the Integrated Nutrition and Health Action Programme (INHAP) was anchored at the VASCSC. Indu Capoor, who had done her Master's in Foods and Nutrition from the Maharaja Sayajirao (MS) University in Vadodara joined the project. At that time, I was the Chairman of the Centre's Standing Committee. It was in that capacity, I came to know her and her work. As I sometimes tell her now "She seemed to be aloof and not very friendly." But one thing was clear: that she managed her project and finances very well and with great discipline.

As the financial accounts of the year 1982-83 were being finalised, they seemed to show that there were accounts receivables in the INHAP project managed by Indu. The senior accountant had brought the statement to me and, knowing Indu and the confidence in her, I was quick to say that this was simply not possible. That discussion led to an investigation, and to the accountant admitting to the fraud committed by him, which was followed by a criminal case.

But that episode also had a silver lining. Based on the experience, we totally changed the accounting and audit systems at NFD. We decided to have an internal audit service which would be common to all the institutions of NFD, at that time, were four.

It was also a period during which I interacted with Indu and came to know of her projects and work. We

saw in those discussions the possibility of creating a new institution with its focus on health and nutrition. The small team of Indu, Minaxi Shukla and Pallavi Naik came up with the name Centre for Health Education, Training and Nutrition Awareness (CHETNA), meaning awareness in several languages.

To start work they needed some space. The VASCSC had a basement which was used for holding temporary exhibitions. We requested Ramesh Kothari, who was then in-charge of the audio-visual and exhibit work, for use of that space. Three months maximum is what he agreed to. Indu and the team completely transformed the place, and work began.

Soon we started searching for a space for the longer term. At that time we had another office behind the screen at the drive-in cinema of Ahmedabad. A full floor was available and I thought this could be transformed into a space for CHETNA. I remember the time we first went there with Indu. She had tears in her eyes as the place was a complete mess. But very soon it was cleaned up and once again transformed into a positive space and a cheerful office facility. Located behind the screen, we used to joke that they were '*parde ke peeche!*'

Founder CHETNA team members with the supportive trustees of Nehru Foundation for Development Mrinaliniben Sarabhai and Kartikeya Sarabhai and Managing Tustee of Lilavati Lalbhai Trust (Late Shri Shrenikbhai Lalbhai) (1996)

The team moved in on 12th August 1984 and CHETNA was finally launched.

The team grew and over the years CHETNA established itself with strong credentials and a unique work culture. In 1992, an opportunity of moving to a better place arose. Lilavati Lalbhai, sister of Kasturbhai Lalbhai, had desired in her will that her house be used for activities related to women and children. My aunt, Manorama Sarabhai, was involved with the estate and in a discussion with my cousin, Anand Sarabhai, suggested that instead of creating a new institution why not ask CHETNA to operate from that space, as their objective was similar. I discussed this idea with Indu and once again the challenge was taken up in a marvellous way. CHETNA totally transformed the building and in its typical style transformed and put life into the idea and into the physical space. For several years, from 1992 to 2006, CHETNA worked out of this office.

But another emotional moment arrived. Manoramaben was no more. Shrenik Kasturbhai, who was Chair of the Lilavati Lalbhai Trust, and very supportive, spoke to me of the changing times. Some of

the other trustees were not in favour of having CHETNA occupy the place. Lilavatiben's desire of working with the neighbouring slum community had been taken up. But the unease with the new trustees remained. In a one-to-one conversation Shrenikbhai told me it was better to look for an alternative as he did not know how long he would continue as Chair. The CHETNA

CHETNA core team with Managing Trustee Nehru Foundation for Development Late Mrinaliniben Sarabhai addressing concerns of Women's Empowerment with village leaders (1996)

team had poured their heart into the Lilavati house and it was a very difficult moment.

In 1998, Indu married Debashish Nayak, who was deeply involved in the conservation of cultural heritage. He identified a haveli in Khadia which CHETNA could use on some suitable terms. Together we worked out an interesting formula for heritage conservation. If we were to use advance rent upfront for conservation, we could achieve two purposes—have an office space and do conservation work simultaneously. The formula was path-breaking in itself and led to CHETNA finally having two properties in Khadia. In addition to this, in 1997, CHETNA purchased its own third property in the walled city of Ahmedabad.

However, none of these city properties were suitable replacements for the Lilavati Lalbhai bungalow at Shahibaug. Having moved often, CHETNA now wanted a space for its head office which they owned. A new construction was coming up at Vadaj and it was decided to buy a floor there. The CHETNA team had put aside savings, and with some borrowings, was able to make the purchase.

As CHETNA grew, much thinking went into issues

of recruitment policies, performance appraisals, staff evaluations and a forum for internal discussions. The governance model, as it emerged decided that the trustees of NFD would essentially play the role of ensuring autonomy of each institution in the form of appointing governing councils, which would provide larger vision and set governance standards for the institution. The Director would be accountable to the governing council. There were several learning's in the appointment of council members as well. We had learned from the VASCSC experience not to change board members other than those who would not attend or had moved away. This ensured that board members felt comfortable to give critical inputs and have a longer association with the institution.

In 1984, the Centre for Environment Education (CEE) was formed with support from Ministry of Environment & Forests. VASCSC was looking at a new salary structure and placing the staff in grades, which were compatible to those in scientific institutions of Government of India. The question at that time was: should this structure be applied to one particular institution or did we need to bring parity among all the institutions under VASCSC. We decided on parity.

While CEE and VASCSC decided to accept government grants, CHETNA had decided not to get into a grant relationship with the government. It was therefore a major challenge for Indu to accept the risk and pay higher salaries. She took it in her stride and with her discipline in financial management not only paid (and continues to pay) a competitive remuneration, but was also able to generate more surpluses, which were later used to grow CHETNA.

While each institution had its own board and directors, we were looking for a space where we could share ideas among these institutions and bring in synergy. The Nehru Foundation for Development Co-ordination Committee (NFDCC) was formed in 1989 and became a forum for directors to exchange experiences. Several practices, such as those relating to staffing, dealing with government, taxation, service rules, legal aspects, recruitments and governance were discussed.

All of this led to what guides the governance of NFD institutions, by which CHETNA has been influenced and in turn has contributed to immensely by its action. Dr Vikram A. Sarabhai's original dream — of creating an institutional space where those interested in contributing as social entrepreneurs could work and grow — continues to drive us in improving our human and institutional development activities. Indu and CHETNA are prime examples of our success representing a wonderful model of social entrepreneurship, financial discipline, good governance, a strong and focussed programme, and working with a clear vision.

The transition in 2013, with Indu taking on the role of heading CHETNA Outreach to take the message of CHETNA nationally and globally, Pallavi becoming Director and Minaxi as Additional Director, represents the maturity of the organisation. To write this experience and bring out the many lessons for the future of CHETNA, as well as other organisations, especially NGOs is a very important task.

— KARTIKEYA V. SARABHAI

Managing Trustee
Nehru Foundation for Development (NFD)

Acknowledgements

This work owes much to CHETNA's Governing Council Members, particularly Kartikeya V. Sarabhai and A.R. Nanda, who were the first ones to encourage me to write about my journey of CHETNA. Many current and former governing council members agreed to interviews and penning their thoughts on their association with CHETNA and my leadership, which has greatly enhanced this book.

I am extremely indebted to Dr. Rajesh Tandon, President, Society for Participatory Research in Asia (PRIA) who spared many valuable hours guiding and mentoring me through the process of writing. He not only provided an enabling space in his beautiful office for me to sit and write on my visits to New Delhi, he also asked me several critical questions which helped me reflect on my childhood experiences, education, family influences and mentors. Being an expert in organisational management, he suggested relevant secondary resource materials to read, which made me think on how I had built and managed CHETNA.

This book, indeed my journey with CHETNA, would not have been possible without the support of my family, particularly my parents. I spent several mornings with my mother before going to meet Rajesh, asking her questions. Her thoughtful answers gave me an insightful peek into my childhood. Debashish Nayak, my husband and soul mate, your support and patience is invaluable as always, especially when I travelled continuously in the months it took to write this book.

My request for narratives on CHETNA and aspects of gender sensitive leadership yielded about 200 analytical and appreciative pieces from CHETNA's former and present team members, partners and well-wishers from India and abroad. All of them have been an integral part of my journey. I am grateful to each one of them, though only a fraction of them are explicitly mentioned in the book.

Pallavi Patel and Minaxi Shukla, my co-travellers

and partners in nurturing CHETNA to become a credible and internationally recognised organisation. Without your passion, dedication and commitment to the cause, CHETNA would not have achieved such heights.

I would also like to thank Anil Gajjar, graphic artist at CHETNA; Di Surgey and the ARROW team, who spared valuable time to explore organisation archives and dig out photographs; and Mansi Shah, for patiently formatting the manuscript and incorporating all my innumerable changes and rewrites.

Kartikeya Sarabhai, Ashoke Chatterjee, Sushmita Ghosh, Dr. Leela Visaria, Usha Rai, Pallavi Patel, Minaxi Shukla and Di Surgey reviewed the manuscript at different stages. Their valuable feedback, comments and suggestions have made this a far better book.

This book, my journey, would not have been possible without the help, guidance and support of all those who have been, and continue to be, a pivotal part of my life. Thank you.

Introduction

Nearly a year ago, one afternoon while sitting in my cabin at the CHETNA office in Ahmedabad, I saw the new director Pallavi (a founder member of CHETNA) feeling somewhat flustered with the various requirements of her new role. She was trying to juggle 'several balls in the air'. Two thoughts crossed my mind. First, I felt great empathy for her. I had stepped out of the role of founder-director of CHETNA a couple of years ago. I knew where the shoe pinched. Second, it dawned on me that I had handed over the leadership of an organisation — CHETNA — that had been birthed and raised to the best of my capacities, and nurtured it in ways that I thought appropriate at various stages of its growth and development. But, I had never shared the full story of CHETNA's organisational evolution, growth and development, and my own learning's in doing so. It seemed only fair that I should complete my 'hand over' by also sharing my own learning's, reflections and insights with the future generation of young leaders and others in similar situations, today and tomorrow.

Encouraged by the managing trustee, our partners, governing council members and a few friends, I embarked on this journey. I decided to pen down my story of building CHETNA as a development organisation dedicated to improving the health and nutrition of marginalised children, young people and women in India, and beyond.

Though experienced, over three decades, to reflect and write about nutrition and health issues of children and women, I had not really written organisational stories. I had contributed my experience at board meetings and to the publications of other organisations.[1]

---

1. Asian-Pacific Resource and Research Centre for Women (ARROW) (*www.arrow.org.my*) is a regional non-profit women's NGO based in Kuala Lumpur, Malaysia. Since 1993, it has been working to advance women's health, affirmative sexuality and rights, and to empower women through information and knowledge, evidence gathering, advocacy, capacity building, partnership building and organisational development. I contributed to the ARROW Resource Kit (ARK) on organisational practices as a board member of ARROW for six years.

I had shared my experiences with colleagues and fellow travellers of development in workshops and informal conversations, but never really sat down to write about my own organisational journey. Therefore, the task of putting down on paper my reflections about building and nurturing CHETNA as a civil society organisation seemed somewhat daunting. What is the story of CHETNA as an organisation? How is it different from the stories of its programmes and activities? Is CHETNA as an organisation really worth writing about? What is distinctive about CHETNA? Haven't such stories already been told before?

With such questions and doubts in my head, I decided to have a conversation with my dear friend, mentor and co-traveller Rajesh Tandon, founder-president of Society for Participatory Research in Asia (PRIA) based in New Delhi. He had been a student of organisational development and had done some writing on this theme himself. I visited him at PRIA in Delhi, spread over six months, and we would chat about my experiences. He would share his experiences in building and nurturing PRIA. Our conversations began to take on a life of their own.

In the course of these conversations, a pattern seemed to emerge in my reflections and writings about CHETNA as an organisation. It began to emerge that there were certain unique ways in which CHETNA was founded, built and nurtured. Several of its values, principles and ways of functioning evolved in practice around gender sensitive issues in organisational life. As a civil society organisation, dedicated to improving standards of nutrition and health for marginalised and disadvantaged children, young people and women, it seemed natural to build the functioning of CHETNA around clear gendered perspectives.

When I began to write about such organisational orientations of CHETNA, I was not sure if there was a theoretical relevance to this aspect of CHETNA as an organisation. As I was not primarily a student of organisational structures, processes and practices, and my reflections on CHETNA were entirely based on own practical insights and experiences, I hesitated to focus on the engendered nature of CHETNA as an organisation. Will this be relevant to Pallavi and others who would be steering the ship of CHETNA after her?

Will this be of interest to any set of readers? Is there any theoretical resonance to these frameworks of organisational understanding and development?

In conversations with Rajesh and other colleagues, I decided that this perspective is uniquely CHETNA's trajectory, and my own lived experience of building and nurturing this organisation over more than three decades. However, it implied that I had to dig deep inside my own self to discover various motivations that shaped my ways of approaching day-to-day functioning of CHETNA. When it became clear that my own leadership had been such a significant influence in the ways in which CHETNA has been shaped over the years, I had to confront my own self to understand my leadership styles. I had not realised that leadership is so closely linked to the personality and motivations of leaders. In order to describe my values and styles of leadership in CHETNA, I had to un-pack my entire life experiences. When confronted with the question 'why this way?', I had to fall back on influences that had shaped me and my upbringing.

I was not sure if my story was indeed so closely related to CHETNA's story. It felt somewhat uncomfortable to talk about my childhood and student days in order to uncover my values, principles, styles and behaviours. I did realise though that I had brought myself, with all my strengths and weaknesses, in founding and building CHETNA. So, I have shared in this book about CHETNA's organisational story several stories of my own past, the choices I made at various stages of my life before and during CHETNA, and the people who were influential in my life. I have decided to share my family, friends and colleagues, their motivations and ways of living, as part of the story of CHETNA.

It is only in narrating these influences that I discovered why and how CHETNA was built as a gender sensitive organisation. The rationales behind organisational choices, ways of taking decisions, nurturing teams of strong women at the top of the organisational hierarchy, taking stands with external stakeholders (government and donors especially) — all this made sense to me after uncovering influences that have been shaping my life and work.

Therefore, this book is as much about me as it is about CHETNA. It is about Indu-in-CHETNA as a uniquely shaped organisation that has clear engendered work spaces, policies, structures, practices and procedures. It is about taking strong feminist leadership to build and run a civil society organisation efficiently that has acquired huge credibility and reputation as an organisation. It is about a founder-leader moving on after three decades at the top of the organisation, and supporting the next generation of leadership to take charge.

It is in this sense that the reflections and stories in this book may make sense to young women and men trying to create 'start-ups', and provide leadership to the next generation of social change organisations in India and beyond. If this book can inspire and motivate the new younger generation leaders and many others struggling to keep development organisations afloat, I would feel gratified with my efforts in realising this book.

Happy reading!

INDU CAPOOR

SECTION ONE

Becoming Indu

1

Independence is key

"Indu! Indu! *Jaldi karo*. We'll be late for the doctor's appointment."

I could hear my mother calling me, but continued to linger in my room, hoping she would leave without me. My younger sister, Jyoti, lived with the effects of polio. She needed constant medical care, and my parents focused their attention on her. Being two years older, I was expected to take care of Jyoti too, especially in the absence of my mother. I regularly took her for physiotherapy sessions at the hospital, which affected my studies to a large extent. Why is it that we think girls sacrificing their play time and putting aside school work to take care of a younger sibling happens only in poor families? This expectation of caring for my

My beautiful mother

younger sibling continued throughout my childhood, into my teenage years. During this period I felt I was neglected to a large extent. I grew up an introvert, preferring to stay in my room and read books, rather than go out and play.

If you know me, you'll be surprised by this statement. Indu the introvert is not the image most people have of me. They see me as a fighter, always ready to make a point on issues that are dear to my heart. I have travelled the world, making presentations and giving speeches in front of large audiences. When my parents shifted to Delhi, I stayed back in Ahmedabad, a single working woman in the late 1970s. I became Director of CHETNA in the early 1980s, and have led the organisation for more than 30 years.

When did 'introvert' Indu become 'independent' Indu?

•

Looking back, I can see I owe a large part of this to my mother, Usha Capoor.

Generally in India, people talk of their mother in

terms of being dependent, submissive and gullible. My mother however is spirited, independent and assertive taking speedy decisions. She was very popular with all, young and old (my father often remarked that she would win any election hands down). All the kids from our neighbourhood and our extended family would love to visit as she always created games and adventures at home. We would build tents in the garden and spend nights there. It was at her insistence that we travelled by road to hill stations and to Chandigarh or Ajmer to visit my grandparents. She wanted us to see a different India from the city we were growing up in. She wanted her children, especially her girls, to be open to experiences.

My mother refers to herself as a 'tomboy' when she was growing up. The fifth child (among eleven children), she played cricket with her brothers, rode a cycle into town to pay the electricity bill and even beat up (or threatened to) her younger brothers' classmates if they dared bully them. She was very popular too. Crowned Miss Shimla when she was studying in college, she was the star attraction at family weddings, singing and dancing to Punjabi folk tunes.

My mother's beauty and vivacity is what made my father seek her hand in marriage. In a scene straight out of a Bollywood film, my father saw her sitting next to the girl whom he had actually come to see as a prospective bride, and was smitten. He told his parents he would like to marry my mother, in spite of the fact she is from Punjab and my father was from Uttar Pradesh. She chose my father as she saw in him integrity and was impressed by my father's profession. My father, Harkrishanlal Capoor, was from the first batch of the Indian Administrative Service (IAS) after independence, an officer from a time when they all considered themselves to be true public servants.

After getting married, my mother joined my father in Mount Abu. They lived in tents, as there was no infrastructure in the districts at the time. My father would leave home early in the morning, often returning late after his tours. My mother is an outdoor, peoples' person. Not satisfied to simply stay at home and be the 'memsahib', she channelled her leadership qualities in social work. She is also very religious. I remember coming home from school on many occasions to find she was not at home because she had gone to listen to a religious discourse. She continued these outings till she was no longer physically able to.

I grew up seeing her use her organising skills to help the less fortunate; she has an innate ability to empathise, be it young or old, rich or poor. Even today, though she is in a wheelchair, she is always ready to help those who come to her in need. It was surprising to me that such an energetic, intelligent woman did not go out of the house to work. Years later, when I started working, I asked her why.

"Your father did not want me to," she told me. "He was afraid that people might ask favours through me. And it was not easy for me to go against his and my in-laws' wishes." It was hard for me to hear this side of my father, a man whom I saw as someone who never stopped his daughters from doing what they wanted to simply because they were girls. In fact, unlike most Indian fathers, he never worried about getting us married.

"Between his work and playing bridge, he never had the time to look for suitable boys for you," my mother laughed. "And I never wanted my daughters to simply look after a family. Which is why I always told the three of you, study hard and get a job, don't be dependent on a man. Independence is key if women are to be treated as equals".

How can I be anything but 'independent' Indu? My mother nurtured her daughters to be self-sufficient, strong, independent individuals, to think of those less privileged than us and to give back to society. This has enabled us to think 'beyond ourselves' and reach out to the more disadvantaged sections of society. My mother inspired, and continues to inspire, me to work towards women's emancipation and empowerment.

2

Socialisation and role models

Although we are four siblings — one brother and three sisters — I grew up in a household only with my sisters. My brother, Ashok, was sent away to a posh boarding school when he was 7 or 8 years old. My father's government salary was certainly not enough to afford this; my grandparents chipped in, but would do so only for the male child! Possibly the only overt gender discrimination I faced growing up. We would meet my brother during school vacations and because he lived away from home, he was quite pampered, not only by my parents but also by my grandparents and his sisters!

With us girls, my mother was a strict disciplinarian. She influenced and dominated the decisions taken at home. There was not much scope to refuse once she

Happy childhood with sisters

had decided what was to be done. My reaction to her dominance was to become more assertive and I would often get reprimanded by her for this. "*Zid mat kar*" (Don't be stubborn), she would admonish me, but later she applauded me for my assertiveness and sticking to my decisions. In fact, she believes that creating CHETNA was the result of my assertiveness — I had refused to get married at an early age to a boy chosen by her (as is the custom in Indian society).

My father retired as Chief Secretary of Gujarat, but till very late in his career we did not realise that he was an important person. To us, he was caring, soft-spoken, humorous, gentle Daddy. My friends wouldn't believe that it was my mother who disciplined us and my father who nurtured us; they had different stories to tell about their own fathers.

My father instilled in us the value of integrity and the courage to speak the truth, especially in a crisis, by his actions. He never misused the office vehicle. Even though he was the top bureaucrat of the state, my mother would travel by public transport to do her shopping and we would travel to college by bus. The bus stop in fact was right opposite the official residence for the Chief Secretary. Though he was very fond of his occasional drink, I have never seen him partake alcohol in Ahmedabad as there is prohibition in Gujarat. In fact, he did not allow my brother to drink at home.

He valued his own and other's time. He was never late for any event, especially when he was the chief guest. He taught us to listen to others, be modest about our achievements, treat all people with respect (including children) and, above all, always see the humour in any situation, particularly in difficult circumstances.

His way of teaching was to narrate stories and incidents, and he encouraged us to read books. Being a gold medallist in English Literature from Allahabad University he was an avid reader himself. Our home was filled with books.

But his most important gift was teaching me persistence and patience in the wake of adversity. I vividly remember that every time I would come back from the field, frustrated about something, he would encourage me to see the brighter side of things. Once I came back crying, complaining how many people were criticising me and I felt everyone was against me. He actually started smiling and said, "Indu, you have arrived, because when you do something worth noticing, that is when people criticise you." Till date, I remember those words, particularly when I face challenges and frustrations.

He was very keen that at least one of his children join the civil services; however, none of us obliged. He tried to convince me that as an IAS officer I would have maximum space to bring about change because there would be access to committed resources; no government officer has to take a 'begging bowl' to a funding agency. But I knew I was far too independent minded and would not be patient with ministers calling on a daily basis to get officers to bend the rules. My father never gave in to such pressure (as a result he was transferred every few years, and sometimes within months of a new posting).

•

Very few of my friends and colleagues know that I was intended to be adopted by my paternal uncle (*chacha*) when I was born as he did not have children of his own. My parents had promised to give me to him as they already had two children (a boy and a girl). *chacha* and *chachi* came all the way from Calcutta (now Kolkata) to Jamnagar, in Gujarat, where I was born. However, my father changed his mind, but till *chacha* passed away, he always treated me as special.

Learning from my two fathers (Chacha and Daddy)

My father was in the civil services while *chacha* worked in the private sector. Both brothers had brilliant careers. Chacha retired as the Managing Director of Dunlop India. I spent many winter vacations with him in Calcutta. The corporate life was completely different from that of a government servant.

In essence, I had two 'fathers' to learn from. While I learnt the importance of values in governance and administration from my father, I learnt leadership and crisis management from my *chacha*, as I watched him deal with labour unrest and crisis in the Dunlop factory.

My bua (father's sister) was another important influence on my choice of profession. She was a doctor, and I have seen her tend to the sick and infirm. She opened my eyes to the nutritional challenge in the country, and how nutrition and health are closely linked. While I knew I did not want to become a doctor, I cannot help but think that my decision to study nutrition was perhaps in some way linked to my conversations with *bua*.

•

The kind of socialisation we experience and the role models we see when growing up cements the attitudes we bring in to the workplace. The egalitarianism between my parents when I was growing up is the kind of equality between men and women which I have unconsciously nurtured in engendering the workplace at CHETNA. The discipline instilled both by my mother and father has helped me tremendously in administration. Many of my father's colleagues have remarked that I am exactly like Capoor *sahib* — efficient in administration with a no-nonsense attitude — which makes me very proud of his legacy.

But the crowning moment of my father's pride in my work was when the UNICEF Chief, on being introduced to him at the Delhi Golf Club, said, "Don't tell me, you are Indu Capoor's father!"

3

Finding my calling

In 1973, having just completed high school from Carmel Convent, New Delhi, I decided to learn music at the Triveni Kala Sangam while I waited for my results. Evenings were spent playing badminton and going for theatrical performances at the Sriram Centre. I was keen on becoming a performing artist (actress) and was trying to convince my parents about my aspiration to get admission to the Film and Television Institute of India (FTII) in Pune or the National School of Drama (NSD) in Delhi. I was however making little progress.

As I had some spare time in the mornings, I decided to accompany my mother on the visits she made almost every day to the neighbourhood slums. She supervised the distribution of milk to children living in the slums on her visits. The conditions in the slums were an eye opener for me. Why do some children not get enough food to eat? What is poverty and why does it exist? How was the milk my mother was distributing going to help? At the dinner table, I would ask my father such questions. My father at the time was posted in the Planning Commission, where the Integrated Child Development Scheme (ICDS)[1] was being formulated. He would patiently explain the context of hunger and poverty in India and how this affected the cognitive and physical development of young children, of how nutrition of young children was a key issue that India faced in developing human capital.

Discussions with my father on the food insecurity of young children prompted him to focus my attention on making a career choice in Food and Nutrition Sciences. At first, I was reluctant, but my father counselled me

1. Launched in October 1975, Integrated Child Development Services Scheme is the world's largest and most unique programmes for early childhood development. ICDS is the foremost symbol of India's commitment to her children — India's response to the challenge of providing pre-school education on one hand and breaking the vicious cycle of malnutrition, morbidity, reduced learning capacity and mortality, on the other.

that this applied science would be the perfect choice for me as he had observed my growing interest in trying out new recipes at home and my concern for poor children, hunger and poverty.

I enrolled in the Bachelor of Science (BSc) Honours (Foods and Nutrition) course offered by Delhi University. There were two colleges in Delhi offering the course at the time. One was Lady Irwin College and the other was a new college, the Institute of Home Economics (IHE) in South Extension. Naturally, my family wanted me to study in the 'prestigious' Lady Irwin College; however, my average performance in the Indian School Certificate (ISC) examinations ensured that I got admission in the IHE.

IHE had not yet gained the credibility and popularity it enjoys today. We were a very small batch and as the college needed to gain credibility, a lot of attention was given to our academic learning. In spite of the heavy course load, I thoroughly enjoyed my time there. I made two very good friends (who remain my best friends till this day). The three of us were always together, taking part in plays and fashion shows, attending musical and theatrical performances. We were constantly 'advised' by our teachers against being 'outspoken and independent', and not to be so interested in fashion and extracurricular activities. Which is why they were shocked when they saw our academic results. All three of us were toppers, and I received the Weikfield Trophy for the Best Student in Foods and Nutrition. My parents (particularly my father) were extremely proud as I had been an average performer in school. I seemed to have found my passion.

Armed with a newly-gained self-confidence, I decided to pursue a Master's degree and my parents wholeheartedly supported and encouraged me.

•

The choice for postgraduate studies was between Lady Irwin College, New Delhi and Maharaja Sayajirao University (MSU) in Baroda, which had a great reputation for its community work. I made a difficult but conscious decision to go to Baroda. This was the first time I was going to stay away from home. There were great challenges in choosing to live in Gujarat in a hostel at the age of 17, particularly since I did not know the local language, but it turned out to be a great learning opportunity. What made it easier was that my two friends also opted to pursue higher studies in Baroda. We decided to share a room. The course work was challenging, which meant we had to work extremely hard, sometimes through the night, but this did not deter us. We somehow also found the time to see movies and plays.

In my first year in the hostel, I was elected as the Food Secretary and in the second year as Entertainment Secretary. As Food Secretary, I was responsible to improve the food served in the hostel canteen. We soon became extremely popular and the three of us came to be known as the Delhi Terrific Trio. Education in Delhi University had given us an edge over the other girls who had graduated from Gujarat.

In the final semester we had to select a topic for our thesis. I was extremely keen on community work, and I wanted to work under the newly appointed head of department, Dr Tara Gopaldas, who had gained recognition in the field of community nutrition. She had overseen Project Poshak in Madhya Pradesh,[2] in which she had developed the take-home food ration concept.

She agreed to be my advisor for my thesis topic on developing anthropometric standards for young privileged Gujarati boys, building on her hypothesis that the World Health Organisation (WHO) standards were not appropriate for Indian children. She was keen to develop Indian standards. This was part of a larger international effort. It gave me an opportunity to stay in an elite boy's residential school for children of Gujarati origin whose parents resided in Africa and America. I was now seeing the other side of the inequities that exist in our society, a stark contrast to the extreme poverty I had seen in the slums on my visits with my mother.

•

2. Project Poshak, conducted in 1971-1975 in the state of Madhya Pradesh, India, was an experimental programme to determine if and when feeding programmes for pre-school age children and pregnant/nursing women could be expanded rapidly, especially in remote rural areas where daily feeding at village day-care centre's was not feasible.

My post graduation years in MSU were extremely educative in different ways. I realised that I loved being independent and my desire to work for the poorer communities became stronger. My experience of studying with Dr Tara Gopaldas was very fulfilling and I say without hesitation that she is my guru.

I did not like biochemistry and laboratory experiments that were part of the course, though I did fairly well in them. I was more interested in community nutrition and I spent time with Dr Gopaldas discussing

Receiving the Outstanding Alumnus Achievement Award-1999-2000 Maharaja Saiyajirao University, Baroda

her experiences. While there were other good teachers in the university, she brought in a rare community experience which made my learning more meaningful. I was lucky when she agreed to guide me through my MSc thesis work. She would spend hours with me, narrating her field experiences and brainstorming. In fact, she was very keen (as was my father) that I should pursue a PhD. She was enthusiastic to guide me as her first PhD student in MSU. But I did not want to become a teacher or professor, which appeared to me the only career avenues open if I did a PhD. I wanted to do something different.

It was Dr Gopaldas who guided me towards serious community work and was instrumental in turning my interest in community nutrition into a passion. The passion I bring to my work in the areas of nutrition and health education is a result of her nurturing. Even when I did not have high self-esteem and confidence in myself, she was optimistic that I would definitely achieve success. She keeps in touch with me and is extremely proud of my achievements. As my '*guru dakshina*'[3], I continue to bring to policy makers' attention her 'pet' mission of making food-based Amylase Rich Food (ARF) protein available to malnourished infants and children.

3. *Guru dakshina*: a gift to a teacher.

SECTION TWO

The World of Work

4

The transparent lesson

I chose to go back to Ahmedabad to be with my parents when I finished my Master's Degree. I was on the lookout for jobs when a family friend's daughter, who was working at the National Institute of Design (NID), offered me a short assignment to re-design the NID canteen. I grabbed the offer as it gave me an opportunity to work in an artistic environment. I spent six months at NID trying to convince designers and artists to remove fried foods from the menu and to change the colour of the table tops (the table tops were black in colour and this attracts mosquitoes). All my analytical nutrition and design advice fell on deaf ears. Samosa's and bread pakoras remained on the menu, eaten at tables with black table tops. My visible successes may have been limited, but the invisible learning, of negotiating skills and conducting oneself in meetings, was incalculable.

My luck changed the day I saw an advertisement posted by CARE, Gujarat, for a nutritionist to evaluate their Supplementary Nutrition Programme (SNP). I responded to the advertisement and was selected for the post. The evaluation was to be anchored by the Vikram A. Sarabhai Community Science Centre (VASCSC), and so that was where I presented myself in March 1980. I was asked to report to the Scientist (Monitoring and Evaluation) who was leading the evaluation.

The evaluation design 'simulated' a supplementary feeding centre in VASCSC itself, where poor children from nearby urban slums were invited to partake of a meal of bread and milk. The children would be engaged in educational activities to keep them occupied and during this I was to observe any behaviour change as a result of the meal that was given. Minaxi Shukla, chemistry major, working in Biology Laboratory was a volunteer, helping to develop and organise nutrition education activities for the children.

The relevance of this monitoring and evaluation (M&E) design puzzled me from the start, but I decided to observe the activities before raising any questions. Within a few days I knew I had to speak up. The purpose of the evaluation of SNP was to assess whether the food meant for children in rural and tribal areas was reaching them. How was a 'simulation' with urban children who were given processed bread and milk going to evaluate this?

I approached the Administrator of CARE to discuss what I thought was a completely wasteful evaluation exercise. I wanted to visit the actual field sites where the programme was being implemented in order to evaluate the extent of outreach of the programme. He was extremely sceptical of the idea of a young woman travelling alone to rural and tribal areas, but once again my stubbornness, as it had countless times in my childhood, asserted itself. Seeing I was not to be deterred, he agreed, as long as I accompanied the CARE officers when they travelled to the field. I raised no objection to this, and thus began my first lessons in transparency and reporting.

First field trip to Dahod, Panchmahals, Gujarat to understand needs (1984)

My field trips to interior areas of Gujarat brought forth a set of realities and experiences which I was completely unprepared for. All young, motivated researchers experience this 'shock' — reality is nothing like the theory that one studies. I entered the field expecting that the supplementary food supplied under the programme would have reached all the target villages (at the time of the evaluation the project was being implemented for three years in 100 villages) where children below 3 years (the target 'beneficiaries') were fed the supplementary food. Imagine my bewilderment when I observed that in majority of the field sites the supplementary food was being fed to cattle and widows, and not to the children. Where the food was being given to children, I was appalled to see that often it was stale food.

Every evening when I returned to the rest house after a long day in the field, I stayed up late into the night writing copious notes of my field observations. This is a habit I have never given up. Writing experiences and observations when they are fresh in our mind brings out minute details, which become hazy, or one even forgets them altogether, as days pass. As they say, the devil is in the details.

On my return to Ahmedabad, I appraised the Administrator about what I had observed in the field. He brushed aside my 'findings' and concerns. When

Donning a saree for the field training in a tribal area of SEWA Rural at Jhagadia Gujarat (1981)

I look back, I wonder: Was he being paternalistic? Having humoured me by allowing me to visit the field, he was now not going to pay any more attention to the issue. How many men behave this way even today, brushing aside ideas simply because they come from someone young, and a woman?

Additional staff were being recruited to implement the project. Pallavi Naik, who was my junior in MSU, joined as a project assistant. Minaxi Shukla too was slowly becoming interested in nutrition issues. I travelled extensively, and used my learning's from each field trip in the development of need-based education material with the help of Pallavi and Minaxi. This was when I first encountered the dearth of awareness at all levels (policy makers, practitioners and communities) on the need for and issues concerning nutrition, or indeed any other developmental goal. There were several good government policies and programmes in place but community awareness severely restricted their reach. On the other hand, policy makers rarely consulted poor, vulnerable and marginalised communities about their concerns which led to development of unrealistic policies and programmes, designed in an international office in New Delhi or the US, with limited impact.

In my spare time, I documented my findings related to SNP based on my field trips. I shared my observations in an in-house newsletter created by me "From the Horse's Mouth". I wonder how many organisations give space to a young, new employee to voice their opinion on how a project is being implemented. I was lucky, in that respect. Perhaps no senior person actually read the newsletter!

A senior person on whom I was making an impression was Kartikeya Sarabhai, the Managing Trustee of the Nehru Foundation for Development (NFD), the umbrella Trust which manages the VASCSC. He would often visit VASCSC for meetings. We did not interact formally, but would pass each other in the corridor. He got the impression that I was extremely arrogant, as I usually walked past with my head held high. Little did he know that I shy away from approaching and talking informally with those whom I do not know personally.

My first formal meeting with Kartikeya was not a particularly auspicious one. He had been shown a few vouchers by the Director of VASCSC which I had signed and on the basis of which 'double payments' had been made by the accountant. This essentially meant that financial expenses were being approved and payments were being made twice to the same party. To date I am not sure why Kartikeya felt I could not have signed those vouchers knowingly, which is why he called me to his office to seek my clarification. I certainly had not benefited from approving those expenses, and offered to go through all vouchers to find where the errors had occurred. For ten days, Kartikeya, the accountant and I sat together in a room sorting vouchers. One day, since I had not brought lunch from home, I went out to buy lunch. I bought bhel puri[4] for myself and the accountant. When I gave the accountant the snack, he looked at me and started weeping. I was surprised by his reaction, and asked him what the matter was. He did not say anything. But through the rest of the day I could see he was disturbed. By evening, he confessed to Kartikeya of embezzling lakhs of rupees from project funds and that he had been doing so for three years! When CHETNA was being set up, I learned from this how important it is for an organisation to ensure that

4. Bhel Puri: A popular savoury snack eaten all over India.

financial records are transparent, clean and monitored regularly.

Many years later Kartikeya told me that in those ten days we spent sorting vouchers, he came to realise that I was simple, sincere, trustworthy, committed, hardworking and friendly! He saw in me a potential to build something when I didn't know that I wanted to set up and lead an organisation. Over the years, he has never interfered in my decisions, and has always supported my professional growth and development. In fact, it was he who convinced me to take a break after 10 years of continuous work to enrol in a three month Certificate Course on Public Health in Developing Countries at the Boston School of Public Health. I had resisted as I was concerned about CHETNA's survival. He knew that my absence would prove how strong the foundation that I had laid was.

In hindsight, I would have been satisfied working quietly, but I am grateful for his motivation and encouragement that made me dream big and allowed CHETNA to grow.

5

CHETNA is born

How could one have imagined that in the span of three and a half decades, this organisation would have grown like this? CHETNA has not only reached out to thousands with its health education, it has also empowered women into a different way of thinking. This could not have happened without leadership. CHETNA is what a vision can do, where a dream can end up.

— Ramesh Menon, award winning journalist and Managing Editor, *India Legal*

I was not content merely writing my observations of the Supplementary Nutrition Programme (SNP) in the in-house newsletter. I strongly felt the need to share my insights with others outside the project team, which led me to write up a formal evaluation report.

The CARE Administrator did not give much importance to the report. I then decided to take matters into my own hands, cyclostyling 100 copies of the report and posting them to government officials and funding agencies, including USAID in America, which was CARE's official donor. I was aware of the consequences of my action and was ready to quit the job if asked to. Was I able to take this step because I come from a privileged background and did not 'need' the salary? (I was living with my parents in Ahmedabad.) Would I recommend this course of action to young employees who have families to take care of, responsibilities to fulfil, for which they need their salaries? My answer is an emphatic, 'Yes'. Don't remain quiet if you are aware of something that is not right in your organisation. Build the courage to speak the truth, especially in a crisis.

My evaluation created quite a stir in the corridors of power as I reported pilferage of oil and bulgur wheat, particularly at the *sarpanch's* (village head) and helper's house, feeding of non-beneficiaries (widows and older children), etc. The report landed on the table of Dr Mary Ann Anderson, nutritionist at USAID in

America, who later travelled to Ahmedabad and asked me to accompany her to the field. In my report I had proposed an integrated comprehensive nutrition and health education programme based on the hypothesis that providing food alone cannot solve the problem of malnutrition; a nutrition programme has to include a component of health education. The programme was subsequently launched by CARE. Unfortunately the CARE Gujarat office was later closed down.

The evaluation report was also read by Dr Lincoln Chen, then the representative of Ford Foundation and a friend of Kartikeya's, when he was staying in Ahmedabad over a weekend. He expressed a desire to meet me. It was a Sunday afternoon when I was called to VASCSC to discuss the findings and how I would do things differently. I was quite frank in my critique and outlined what I thought was a better strategy and methodology for a nutrition programme. Lincoln asked me to write a brief concept note for a project based on what I had put forward.

I wrote a note going well beyond the brief of a project proposal. I proposed an institution that would work as a bridge between policy and practice. The idea was based on the premise that for the situation to change, we all — self, community, policy makers and programmatic staff — needed to become conscious at all levels. All of us needed to be aware. *Chetna* means awareness in Hindi and several other Indian and Asian languages, and we came up with the acronym CHETNA, or Centre for Health Education, Training and Nutrition Awareness, for this institution.

Ford Foundation liked the idea and decided to give a bridge grant for six months to the Nehru Foundation for Development (NFD). Kartikeya took the 'risk' of accepting a short-term grant for this work based entirely on my enthusiasm and commitment to create CHETNA. CHETNA was to be housed in, and continues to be part of, NFD. Many people are surprised that CHETNA is not a separate legal entity registered under a relevant Act to form a society or trust. This in no way takes away from CHETNA being an institution, an organisation. It has committed individuals who have come together for common purpose, has an independent governing council and written systems and processes through which it carries out its work. Having passed on the leadership baton, its survival is not dependent on my enthusiasm and commitment alone.

As part of the grant, I was sponsored by Ford Foundation to visit the International Centre for Diarrhoeal Disease Research, Bangladesh (ICDDRB), field site in Matlab, Bangladesh, where Lincoln had implemented a large scale diarrhoea control project using rice based Oral Rehydration Solution (ORS). It was to be a precursor to developing a large field proposal for implementing a child health project in Gujarat.

It was my first 'foreign trip' and I was excited. We visited the most interior areas of Matlab, where hunger and poverty were so severe that I thought it was not real and I was watching a film. Dr Saroj Pachauri, then Programme Officer at Ford Foundation, accompanied me on the trip. This was the first grant she would be handling, and she wanted to be sure of this young, unmarried girl in her 20s. Perhaps her concerns were legitimate as she didn't want the project left in the lurch should I decide this was not the career I wanted.

On our return from Bangladesh, Lincoln, Saroj and I discussed the possibility of replicating the ICDDRB Matlab experience in Gujarat. I didn't think the programme design used in the Matlab model was appropriate for Gujarat as in the intervention sites we were proposing diarrhoea was not the only concern. Acute Respiratory Infection (ARI), malnutrition and anaemia also affected child health in these sites.

Both Lincoln and Saroj were open to an implementation strategy to adopt a comprehensive integrated approach to improving the health of children in Gujarat. I also proposed that the child survival project would not be implemented by CHETNA. Rather, CHETNA would build capacities of field non government organisations (NGOs)/community based organisations (CBOs). This would make the project more sustainable and strengthen community development. This was also based on my experience that due to diverse dialects used in every district (particularly Kutchi) effective grass roots education by any one organisation is a challenge. We proposed the names of about 10 field based NGOs working in the area of health.

The strategy was approved, and I was asked to develop a proposal in collaboration with Gujarat Institute of Development Research (GIDR), Ahmedabad. Late Dr Pravin Visaria, who had recently shifted back from the US, was director at GIDR. CHETNA would build capacities of five or six NGOs to implement the project and GIDR would design and implement the M&E part of the proposal.

Once the joint proposal was submitted and sanctioned, CHETNA was born on 12 August 1984. We were a team of 10 members, including Pallavi, Minaxi, me, the support staff and a driver. We even bought a second hand Fiat for field travel. When we shifted from VASCSC to our own office, in rented premises behind the drive-in cinema, we christened our office space *parde ke peeche* (behind the curtain). An appropriate baptism, since CHETNA went on to work in the area of women's empowerment, lifting the veil they live behind and making their voices heard.

6

A woman at work

Writing my first proposal was an extremely eventful journey during which I experienced a high learning curve. I realised that being young is an advantage as one is courageous, willing to take risks and be frank (or at least I was). But being young, and a woman, can also be a handicap.

The field visits I made with Dr Visaria to collect data as part of the joint project proposal was very challenging. Every time we encountered a mother with a sick child, I would begin counselling her on health and nutrition. He would ask me to stop, as in his view this would 'contaminate' the data we were collecting. Traditional research is based on the premise that the researcher must not get involved with the respondents while the research is being conducted. In my view, especially in the area of health, this seemed unethical, as a young child with diarrhoea can die in two days if the parents lack information on how to take care of the child. How then can we stand apart and say nothing when we see a sick child?

Dr Visaria was already a legend in his area of expertise, demography. As is common with those with formidable reputations at work, peers and colleagues are hesitant to contradict them, or raise questions. Whenever I argued with him on methodological issues, he would quietly but firmly say, “Indu, I finished my Master’s in economics in the year you were born [1957].” Many times he made me cry. Dr Leela Visaria (his wife and presently a member of CHETNA’s board) though would applaud me for having the courage to ask critical, analytical questions.

•

I wasn’t ready for a patriarchal workplace when I began my career. I am from a fairly ‘liberal’ family where girls are not overtly discriminated against. My father was an extremely sensitive and caring man, as is my brother. So when I stepped out of my 'safe zone' (my home) to start working, I must admit to experiencing a culture shock.

It began from the interview for the role of nutritionist in the evaluation project. I was told that one of the reasons I would be given the job is because no male candidate had applied. The Administrator at CARE opposed my going to the field because he was 'worried' how a young, single girl would manage in a village, among a tribal community. When I did go to the field, caretakers at the guest houses we were booked to stay in refused to allot me a room because they had assumed a project officer can only be a man. Tired after an entire day in the field, I had to argue and cajole before they gave me a room. The male field officers would invariably take the better ones.

In the early 1980s, I was often the only woman in the room in policy and programme meetings, and a young woman at that. Making my voice heard was not easy. When CHETNA was established, I was given the title of Director, a title I was not comfortable with. Initially, my response was to don plain glasses and wear a sari to blend in. It took me a long time to accept my designation and the 'power' that was synonymous with it. The designation though was particularly useful in a room full of men, many of them senior policy makers, to get them to take what I said seriously. But what really used to upset me was when people who came to the office, sat in my cabin, listened to the CHETNA story and then asked, "Who is in charge?"

It is so natural to assume that men are the leaders. Many people think that women should not be given opportunities to grow in an organisation and be leaders, because women must be submissive, or because they will anyway get married and then have to look after the family. The patriarchal mindset among men and the socialisation of girls from a young age — to cook, serve and look after the men/boys in the family, to sacrifice their owns desires, not to voice their own opinions, to let men 'take charge' — plays itself out in the workplace. I have worked to build a woman-led organisation; yet this behaviour has often cropped up even within CHETNA.

In spite of being highly educated, women in CHETNA would be deferent when talking to men

regardless of their designation. The men would not respond positively to any requests for work to be done unless they were pleaded with. One of my earliest memories as a leader is when I spoke loudly to an accountant, questioning him because he had made a major mistake, and he began sobbing, loudly, telling me that no woman, including his mother and sister, had ever scolded him. I was aghast and told him that at the workplace he was not going to be treated as anybody's son or brother. He was an accountant and

Main kuchh bhi kar sakti hoon

I had the right to point out his extremely expensive mistake because I was accountable to the funding agency on behalf of CHETNA.

Such socialisation patterns are acute in the health/gender sector in India, especially among female field workers. It takes a lot of effort to build their self-esteem, to enable them to assume and accept leadership. Frontline workers in the health sector, such as Auxiliary Nurse Midwives (ANMs) and Accredited Social Health Activists (ASHAs), carry the maximum burden of work. While a lot of attention is given to developing their technical skills, lack of self-esteem, confidence and time constraints does not allow them to use these skills. They are unable to perform well because of the subordinate status of women within the health system and the communities in which they work. They have to deal with young doctors (generally male) who often 'dump' their medical responsibilities on them while they continue to pursue their postgraduate studies in urban areas. The ideas put forward by female frontline workers, even when based on field experiences, are not valued, yet any opinion given by men (at all levels) is welcomed. In the education sector, Anganwadi Workers

(AWWs) and teachers are constrained to share the food received at Anganwadi's and schools for the Mid Day Meal (MDM) scheme with the *sarpanch*. At home, as daughters and daughters-in-law, they are expected to fulfil all household and child care responsibilities without any support from men, resulting in multiple burdens often leading to ill-health or poor performance.

In a conference, Dr Samir Narayan Chaudhuri, Secretary and Founder Director, Child In Need Institute (CINI), West Bengal, raised the issue why female frontline workers are not able to perform well on the job. He recounted that during trainings at the CINI training centre, ASHAs, ANMs and AWWs usually pick up the concepts extremely well. However, when CINI workers go on field visits as follow-up a few months later, they observe that the same women are not able to perform effectively. The reason is that when the trained woman worker goes back, she has to carry out her traditional roles as well. The time constraint in performing multiple tasks affects her output at work. Boys and men generally do not face such issues.

•

Ila Vakharia was born and brought up in Nagpur, Maharashtra. A dreamer with strong will power, she firmly believes that injustice and discrimination is not acceptable at any cost, which is why she chose to work to empower women.

Ila settled in Nadiad, Gujarat, after marriage. Finding the right job was hard. Then one day she received an interview call from CHETNA. She had no technical knowledge, and wrote her answers to the questions on health and nutrition based only on her common sense of taking care of her family. During the interview, the male committee members were doubtful how she would be able to make the daily commute from Nadiad, particularly since she had a young daughter, but the women members were appreciative when she expressed she was ready to take up the challenge.

Initially, the daily commute and coping with family and the responsibility of a child was hard. The first challenge was that the train timings did not match the office hours (9 am to 5 pm). CHETNA allowed her to come to office a little later (coinciding with the arrival of the train Gujarat Queen) and permitted her to take work home. As health and nutrition was a new subject for her, she spent her commute reading for self-learning.

Her next challenge was when she became pregnant with her second child within a month of joining work. CHETNA did not ask her to quit, as many organisations are prone to do. Six months into her pregnancy, she fell down and injured her leg. Fortunately, the baby was unharmed. In spite of her injury, she fulfilled her responsibility at an immunisation event CHETNA organised at the annual function of Gujarat Voluntary Health Association in Ahmedabad.

Following this, I discussed with her the possibility of working from home during the rest of her pregnancy. I offered her the task of translating the book *Where There is No Doctor* into Gujarati. The book changed Ila's perception of health and medical services, reaffirming her commitment to working in the health sector.

Having delivered a baby, Ila found it was going to be difficult for her to travel leaving her newborn at home. Her husband understood, and decided they would shift to Ahmedabad and he would now start commuting to Vadodara. When she rejoined work, she was conflicted about not being able to breast feed her child. Given that CHETNA promotes breast feeding, she asked for an extended lunch hour during which she could go home and feed her child. CHETNA did not hesitate in supporting her.

Ila worked in CHETNA for 27 years, gaining experience in implementing projects related to children, adolescents and women. She was provided opportunities to enhance skills in the area of advocacy, networking, administration and accounts. She joined CHETNA as a field worker and took voluntary retirement as a senior programme officer. Ila's professional journey would not have been possible without the support of her organisation and her family.

•

Over three decades of building women's leadership in CHETNA, I am convinced that a workplace has to organise work routines around women's body rhythms or life cycle experiences. Often heads of organisations report that marriage and pregnancy interfere with women's organisational duties and leadership potential, but in a gender sensitive organisation these can and should be woven in as opportunities for organisational growth. Appreciation, support and giving women employees the space to grow makes for loyal workers. Many women and men have been working in CHETNA for more than 30 years.

"In 1996-97, CHETNA started its training centre in Desai Ni Pol, Khadia, in the walled city of Ahmedabad. At that time, my second child was six months old. I lived in Khadia and the organisation gave me the administrative responsibility of the training centre as well as providing logistic support during trainings," remembers Arti Trivedi, administrative assistant at CHETNA. "This shows CHETNA's sensitivity to my requirements as a mother. The Khadia training centre was a completely different experience for me. I feel proud that I got the opportunity and I could prove myself".

Developing capacities of women according to their passion has also been CHETNA's strategy from its inception. Pallavi was more interested in women's health and development and a Women's Health & Development Resource Centre (WHDRC) was created at CHETNA, which she led for several years. Minaxi is extremely fond of children and she was given charge of CHETNA's child resource centre. This division of portfolios remained, although the separation of the centres was discontinued many years ago.

When colleagues could not travel due to difficult pregnancies, I saw these as opportunities to expand CHETNA's work in urban areas. We collaborated with Self Employed Women's Association (SEWA) to develop capacities of their health workers in Ahmedabad. Through this exposure, CHETNA gained expertise and experience in working in urban slums. This gave us immense visibility as we developed several training modules which are used not only in India, but all over the world, even today.

Fortunately for CHETNA the issue of sexual harassment at the workplace has never been an organisational concern. But as more women, particularly young women, join the workforce this is an issue organisations will have to address. The Prevention of Sexual Harassment of Women Act was finally passed in 2013 after hanging fire in parliament for over a decade. Nehru Foundation for Development has formed the legally mandated internal complaints committee and has a codified prevention of sexual harassment policy. A gender sensitive organisation must take this issue on board, and make all efforts to create an enabling working environment where women (and men and transgender) feel safe and secure.

7

Knowledge, action and communication

When CHETNA's field staff started training frontline workers and began working with communities, they experienced strong resistance. Communities were not ready to accept the health education that we imparted, which was based on an allopathic perspective. Initially, we assumed that it was their illiteracy that was the barrier to their learning. Slowly we realised that the people themselves are great reservoirs of traditional knowledge. To get them to accept new, scientific knowledge, we first needed to understand their local knowledge and practices. Only then would our actions have meaning and impact.

Spurred by this learning, we undertook a study to document and validate existing beliefs and practices among local communities in collaboration with the Lok Swasthya Parampara Seva Sansthan (LSPSS) who were recognised experts in the field. At the end of the study, we published a book on women's traditional practices for mother and child health entitled: *Her Healing Heritage*. This was a pioneering publication and gave CHETNA a unique identity and visibility.

The study also helped us identify traditional health practices which were useful, and those which were harmful. During our educational sessions with marginalised communities we stressed their beneficial practices, and then explained how the harmful ones needed to be replaced with new practices. Building on traditional knowledge ensured better acceptance by communities who felt valued since their knowledge was recognised. We became more effective in bringing about behaviour changes related to health practices, particularly in tribal areas where access to primary healthcare is poor.

Ila Vakharia, who is a strong believer in traditional health practices, further strengthened our belief and understanding of the link between nutrition and Ayurveda after she attended a workshop. When

CHETNA was asked to anchor an all-India study on local health traditions in the area of maternal and child health, we were open to hiring a *vaidya* (traditional doctor). That is how Smita Bajpai, a trained medical practitioner, joined CHETNA.

Raised in a gender biased north Indian society, Vd. Smita Bajpai resented being discriminated throughout her life on basis of gender. Studying Ayurveda was a challenge and it didn't fit into the image of a *vaidya* being a man. In 1989, Smita was interviewed at CHETNA through a very transparent, fair and competitive process. She got an opportunity to compete with 25 men; some of these candidates were her colleagues. She was selected based on her competencies and qualifications, not because she was a woman. Surprisingly, she was the only one who firmly believed in the ancient science of Ayurveda. Extremely committed to the use of Ayurveda, Smita has contributed to developing CHETNA's understanding of Ayurvedic traditions and integrating it into our field programmes.

CHETNA has provided Smita the much needed experience and exposure on understanding women's holistic health concerns, the feminist approach and space to explore her potential and contribute towards the larger cause of women's empowerment. In her work, she has had several opportunities to apply her learning's from Ayurveda to understand women's healing knowledge, try out various models, and join other women/women's networks to benefit from their knowledge of health and healing. In 1995, CHETNA deputed Smita under a Ford Foundation scholarship at the International Centre for Research on Women (ICRW), Washington, DC, for three months. It was her first trip abroad and gave her an enabling opportunity to link Ayurveda with local health traditions surrounding pregnancy and child birth.

CHETNA has provided Smita a vast canvas to learn, experiment, apply, and grow. She has used those opportunities to establish herself as a *vaidya*, a title she chose, she was motivated and encouraged to introduce herself as a *vaidya* in several public forums and to write her title as Vd. Smita. Even today, people are curious and enquire about her title, which provides her an opportunity to establish herself as a *vaidya*.

In her role as Project Director, she helps her team

mates grow. And the flame of proving herself and changing the stereotype of a *vaidya* being a man continues.

Professor (Dr) G.G. Gangadharan, Director, M.S. Ramaiah Indic Centre for Ayurveda and Integrative Medicine in Bengaluru has been a partner in CHETNA's journey in integrating local health knowledge into our field level actions.

> I had been nursing a dream of turning Ayurvedic principles and theory into action through community health programmes. When I started working in the field, I found how difficult it was to translate theory into action. But then I met Indu and her team at CHETNA. I saw the sound work they were already doing in this area. I worked closely with Indu for 10 years on the Women and Health (WAH!) programme as the only male taskforce member. WAH! was implemented in India to train middle level women health managers. It was Indu who advocated for traditional medicine to be an important component of this training.

What is the purpose of knowledge, of research if there is no action? Any action must give space to customary knowledge, to the wisdom of communities;

which is why, CHETNA blends traditional ways of doing things with modern practices when empowering women to become health leaders in their communities. CHETNA's innovations in improving access to maternal health services using the formal public health system as well as strengthening the role of *dais* (traditional birth attendants) in remote, tribal areas of India created a deep impact on policy in the 12th Five Year Plan.

Sayeda Hameed, former Planning Commission member between 2004 and 2014, believes this is because of CHETNA's understanding of social determinants, particularly gender, and their impact on health of marginalised communities. "Their advocacy for health workers such as *dais*, Auxiliary Nurse Mid-wives (ANMs), Anganwadi Workers (AWWs) and Accredited Social Health Activists (ASHAs), is the fulcrum of their work," she says. "CHETNA has chosen a tough path where results are neither instant nor spectacular. But this is the only path which leads to steady human development".

Communicating health

CHETNA emerged at a time when India was experimenting with creating policies and programmes directed at addressing public health. Was public health about infrastructure, or health services? And what kinds of health messages could link beneficiaries to these services? Sending out such messages was the main task for 'communicators' within the system: messages about the need to limit family size, to avail of systems of maternal care, to ensure essential vaccinations, to drink clean water… the list went on. This remains the mode of communication even after seven decades of message-sending.

CHETNA chose 'social communication', a process rather than an output. It believes that communities, and within them the women, need to be involved in deciding what change should come and how it should come. I asked Ashoke Chatterjee, Former Director, National Institute of Design (NID), Ahmedabad, what he thought about CHETNA's health awareness communication and action. I could not have put it better.

> A dawn drive through rural Rajasthan highlights a challenge that CHETNA has tried to address through all the years of its efforts at health awareness and action. This is the gap between 'talking health' and 'acting health'. On every village wall, official investment in the Swachch Bharat Campaign[5] is evident: slogans freshly painted on the importance of latrine construction. And in every field, along every path, citizens with bottles are on their way to and fro from the morning ritual of open defecation. The gap between 'latrine construction' and 'latrine

5. Swachch Bharat Campaign: Clean India Mission.

use' could not have been more graphically presented, nor the fundamental challenge of so many well-intentioned campaigns over so many decades. That challenge is behaviour change, which understands that the eradication of open defecation is a process that must take place 'between the ears, not between the cheeks'. Why should we need a Swachch Bharat Campaign almost a century after the Mahatma demonstrated his belief that sanitation, and the need to link cleanliness with human dignity, was even more important than freedom?

The answer to that question is linked to CHETNA's experience and effort. The answer comes from listening, a process to which CHETNA has given exemplary attention. Through its work with communities, and most particularly with women, CHETNA has discovered and demonstrated that perceptions of health as communicated from the 'top' may not necessarily match perceptions of health with 'beneficiaries' at the 'bottom'. If size is seen as a poor family's only insurance against infirmity and old-age, why limit families? If a child's faeces, is as innocent as the babe, why all the fuss about hygiene and hand-washing? If cholera or smallpox is a punishment inflicted by divine forces, what can a mere vaccination do to avoid them? If the test of good water is its taste and clarity to the eye, what is the need for other safety measures?

CHETNA's major contribution to social communication has been in its demonstration of communication as a two-way dialogue of building consensus on issues and joint action toward change. This has stood in contrast to the prevailing habit of designing and sending messages one-way in the hope that a message received will be a behaviour changed. CHETNA knows this is not so. It has helped the sector to understand that communication is a social process in which the first step is to develop consensus on the issue and to invest in this long and patient process. Unless the understanding of family wellbeing or personal hygiene is a shared one, no amount of investment can lead to real and lasting change, even if political will prevails at the highest level. Latrines may be constructed with official subsidies, but they will be used as stores, not as toilets. For defecation, the open air (and for women the rare chance to socialise) may continue as the preferred option.

Another truth that has been a foundation in CHETNA's sector leadership has been its understanding of women as the most important and most dependable catalysts for change. CHETNA has helped the country to understand that poor social indicators are most often indicators of societies where women remain at the margins, far too often deprived of their right and capacity to lead change. In every area of CHETNA's health endeavour, the gender factor has been a critical one. Mobilising women in the communication process, as the ones to be listened to before any decision is taken on what has to change and why, has been an important demonstration by CHETNA and through the partnerships it has forged across the country and beyond.

Understanding the importance of communication has also encouraged CHETNA to invest in documenting its experiences, even if aspirations can seem to exceed capacity. The fact that CHETNA takes documentation seriously; has meant the building of an institutional memory bank, a critical factor in its credibility as a trainer and of the communication team that CHETNA has built. From a communication perspective, CHETNA's efforts at recording processes of change and learning from them has been unique in a sector in which communication is still largely understood as media products (rather than the social, behavioural and political changes that media products are supposed to assist) and in which recording of experience is often neglected due to other pressures.

All this has not been easy. The temptation persists, even within CHETNA, to judge communication success by the bulk of print and electronic media products. In the midst of the rapid changes in information technology, the challenge and the opportunity for CHETNA today is to link its grass roots credibility in listening and dialogue with the incredible opportunities which technology and social media now offer. It is institutions like CHETNA, rooted in communities and deriving their credibility from them, that can make the most powerful demonstration of a decentralised, democratic communication system in which development is understood as the ability of the deprived to make intelligent choices. What CHETNA has done and is doing deserves to be appreciated in that context.

SECTION THREE

Building a Gender Sensitive Organisation

8

Locating CHETNA's identity and structure

What kind of an organisation is CHETNA? Is it like most NGOs or is it like a business organisation? I think it seems to have integrated the best of both! Typically, NGOs are seen as being compassionate and socially oriented in their objectives and approach, with a relaxed, creative and informal environment. In sharp contrast, professionally managed 'corporate organisations' are seen as being efficient, productive and result oriented. In CHETNA, Indu and her team have managed to create a beautiful blend of these two styles. In our language at Pragati Leadership, we call this the 'wholesome organisation': One which has managed to harmoniously integrate two apparently opposite styles into something that works for joyful effectiveness.

— Arun Wakhlu, Former Governing Council Member, CHETNA and Executive Chairman, Pragati Leadership, Pune.

When the CHETNA journey began, it was just three of us — Minaxi, Pallavi and myself. By 1984 we had expanded to a team of 10 persons. When it was just the 3 of us, we worked sitting around one large table and our enthusiasm and hard work led to several positive outcomes. We set timings according to our convenience and the temperature, e.g., sometimes in summer we used to begin work at 7:00 am. VASCSC, the institution we were housed in, was an established organisation with rules and regulations, timings, leave rules, etc. Ironically, ours was the most vibrant work centre with the least amount of rules and funds!

During the initial years of CHETNA we struggled to develop a unique identity for ourselves. It was later that we came across Participatory Research in Asia (PRIA), a like-minded organisation in New Delhi, which had expertise in participatory research and training. They undertook capacity building of NGOs through a Training of Trainers (ToT) programme. I nominated all senior trainers at CHETNA for a three-phase ToT conducted by PRIA. I was also very keen to join; however, I could not afford to take time off as I was busy building and managing the organisation.

This ToT proved to be one of the best investments that CHETNA ever made. Dr Rajesh Tandon and late Dr Om Srivastava are not only excellent facilitators but also great human beings, truly interested in building institutional and human capacities of the development sector. As part of PRIA's capacity building processes, leaders are also exposed to a series of seminars and workshops on leadership, which I had the privilege to attend. In this process I engaged with both Rajesh and Om extensively and learnt a lot about adult education and organisational management. I got an opportunity to work with them when Rajesh invited me as a subject specialist to conduct an Early Childhood Care and Development (ECCD) ToT in Malaysia for Bernard van Leer Foundation (BvLF), Netherlands.

The senior team members of CHETNA also attended a Vision, Mission and Strategy workshop conducted by PRIA where we collectively developed CHETNA's vision and mission.

CHETNA's vision

CHETNA envisages an equitable society where disadvantaged communities are empowered to live healthy lives.

CHETNA's mission

> To empower children, young people and women, especially from marginalised social groups, so that they become capable of gaining control over their own, their families' and communities' nutrition, health and wellbeing.

By 2001, CHETNA had established a reputation for teamwork and was widely recognised. We received invitations from all over India to conduct ToTs on health. Our enthusiasm and inner need to respond to every invitation took us to Odisha, Andhra Pradesh and many other states. However, I soon started feeling that we were unable to ensure an impact; the quality of our work was suffering as we were spreading ourselves too thin. I approached PRIA to conduct a strategic review of our work over the past five to ten years.

PRIA's strategic review suggested CHETNA focus on one or two states, have strong long term linkages with government, NGOs and CBOs, and use the experience and evidence gained to advocate for state, national and international policies and programme.

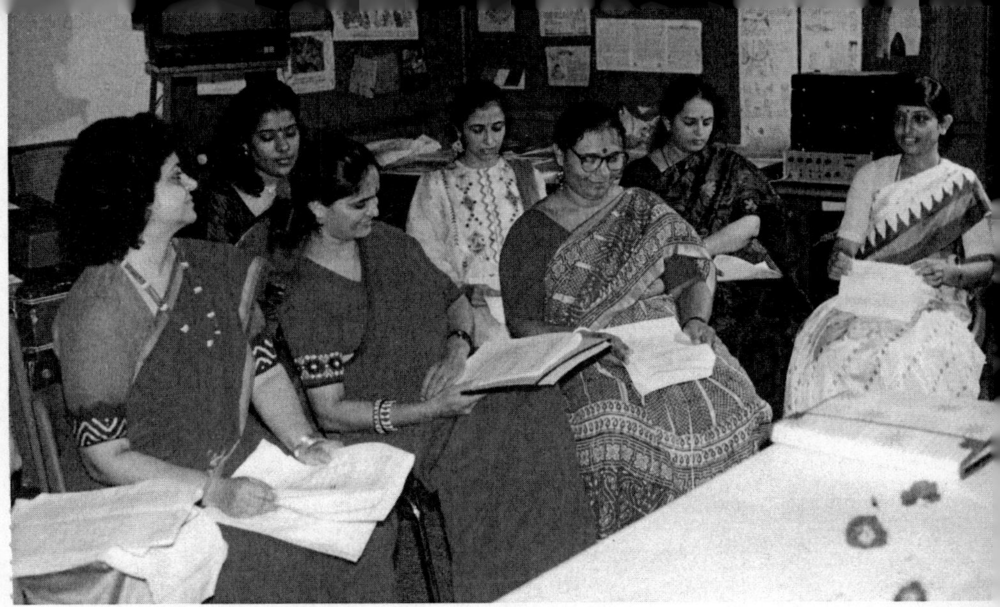

Building a work culture

I remember the relaxed and homely ambience in the CHETNA offices which welcomed visitors and made it a joy to have conversations over masala chai. At one time CHETNA even had a *maharaj* (chef) who cooked up the most delectable Gujarati dishes to feed members of CHETNA and guests.

— Arun Wakhlu, Former Governing Council Member, CHETNA and Executive Chairman, Pragati Leadership, Pune

Celebrating a decade of CHETNA (1990)

As the team grew, it was clear that while they worked on different projects, my primary task was to keep the team motivated, and ensure the flow of communication and synergy among team members. When the need for formal systems arose, I developed organisational work processes and a culture based on what I had observed in both the corporate world and the development sector. While there are many perceived differences between the two worlds, I felt CHETNA should adopt the best of both. Some 'corporate' structuring and decision-making style was necessary for efficient functioning.

The corporate world thrives on quick decision-making, as they know delayed decisions may lead to cost implications, which could ultimately mean loss of profit. The decision is taken at the top and then implemented without question, flowing down the hierarchy. This ensures a clear line of control.

Small NGOs tend to undertake piecemeal decision-making. Many decisions are driven by community needs and the vision/mission of the organisation, and are taken at the level of teams working in the field, which can lead to lack of clarity and chaotic operations.

Decisions are usually delayed due to absence of the leader. No one dares to question the motive of a leader once a decision has been taken.

We did not want to be leader-centric and lose our ability to include people in taking decisions. I wanted the culture and values of the organisation to be based on participatory decision-making, team synergy, equity, principles, appreciation and utilisation of all available talent.

Intuitively, though, I realised that while freedom of decision-making, autonomy of implementation and consultation were extremely necessary to innovate, accountability and transparency were as necessary for survival. One of the systems that were institutionalised was maintenance of time sheets for accountability of plans and financial monitoring of income and expenses in projects. This helped cut down on undue time being spent on activities which can be done more efficiently by others. Learning from the corporate culture, we introduced standard operating procedures for almost all tasks/activities, which led to standardisation of quality/output.

We wanted to innovate, while placing great

emphasis on the process. We eschewed the corporate philosophy of 'output at any cost'. Synergy among teams and individuals was important if I wanted to strengthen a culture of innovation. A monthly team meeting was started where all staff, including administration and accounts, shared their achievements and challenges. When all issues were on the table, decisions would be taken. To ensure that new team members felt part of the organisation, they were encouraged to share their learning's, experiences and challenges in the monthly team meeting. When teams became too large, we introduced the internal newsletter, *CHETNA Update*, where lessons for future work are summarised through documentation and analysis. This internal newsletter is brought out in the first week of every month even today.

I have always believed that human resources, not buildings or vehicles, is the greatest asset in an organisation. People need to feel valued and their talents must be nurtured. The corporate way is to value a worker through the compensation paid. Equally, poor performance is not tolerated. Tightly-drawn contracts are invoked in case of non-performance, and sacking people on short notice is not unusual. In the development sector traditionally, employees are made to feel valued through participation in the decision-making process, by caring for their views and opinions. NGOs can often lay more emphasis on loyalty and commitment, less on output and efficiency. Such practices help in attracting talented human resources, as all individuals have a great need for recognition/appreciation, but it cannot be the reason for low levels of monetary compensation.

We were very clear from the beginning that CHETNA would pay a good salary to all its employees, a level of compensation that would allow us all to maintain a decent standard of living. As far as possible we avoid 'project cycle' based appointments, which affects the morale and security of employees. Adopting some fixed pay rules for core team/regular staff based on government guidelines was a decision made by the Nehru Foundation for Development that increased the loyalty of team members. Salaries were generally higher than other NGOs which attracted talented and committed professionals. Our decision to pay well was also done to avoid moonlighting, which I had observed.

To keep up the morale and motivation, team members were encouraged to articulate their interests, and I made great efforts to actively seek projects in that direction. Consultancy fees that we earn from such assignments are deposited in the common CHETNA core fund. This serves two purposes: building the capacity of staff as well as building long-term reserves for CHETNA.

We have a standardised recruitment system, and while we make special efforts to recruit talented and qualified people, we never compromise on attitude, passion, motivation and commitment. Since our work requires us to interact with marginalised and illiterate communities, these qualities are critical to the selection of CHETNA team members.

Branding of the corporate name is given prime importance for organisational visibility in the private sector; in NGOs, it is often the founder-leader who gets maximum visibility. At CHETNA, visibility is given to teams working in the field. Synergy and cross-learning between different project teams is encouraged and outputs from each team are generously shared. Teamwork is applauded and collaboration, not competition, between teams is the modus operandi. As in all organisations, there is occasional conflict between teams, but this is resolved by timely dialogue and discussions. While teamwork is valued and duly recognised, a performance-based incentive/promotion system is in place.

Attracting and retaining young talent is always a challenge. A common practice in CHETNA is to acknowledge, appreciate and applaud good practices by junior team members. Young employees are mentored and inducted by senior team members, both in field work, documentation and analysis. Investment and trust in younger team members is systematically planned and they are nominated to capacity building opportunities, both internally and externally.

CHETNA's office systems are non-discriminatory, primarily recognising the value of human resources and have been created to promote the values of commitment, honesty, transparency, accountability and enhancement of capacities. We feel proud to say that today almost all development organisations look forward to receiving an employee who has been trained and has worked in CHETNA. When an employee whom we have invested in leaves, it may be a loss to the organisation, but it is definitely a contribution to society.

CHETNA team members who have left the organisation are our ambassadors. We have also welcomed back those who have been disillusioned by the 'outside' world; the job satisfaction they get from working at CHETNA is incomparable, they feel, even if they are working at a lower salary.

> Over the years, I have had many occasions to participate in CHETNA's meetings, field activities and functions. I always got the feeling that CHETNA has managed to evolve a people friendly culture. As an organisation grows and diversifies, the requirement for coordination increasingly becomes stronger. This necessarily implies 'hierarchy', which the Women's Movement had loudly declared as an unacceptable concept. Also, the need to have qualitative refinement in all activities necessitates specialisation and search for expertise. The challenge for CHETNA has been to ensure these management requirements within a framework of 'equality' and 'participation'. The message that we get over the years from CHETNA's management style is that hierarchy has to be distinguished from

domination, and efficiency can be ensured without stiff instruction.

— Dr Sharada Jain, eminent educationist and founding chairperson of CHETNA's governing council.

Organisational structure

Till 1990, CHETNA did not feel the need for a formal structure as we were a small team. The work was divided among the five senior people based on their interests. Pallavi Naik and Jyoti Gade led the women's team and Minaxi Shukla and Ila Vakharia anchored the children's team, with the artists, administration, publications and accounts personnel working with both teams.

This structure continued for quite some time. After a few years, we realised that while division between the women's and children team was useful for functional purposes, it did lead to some conflict. Women and children, particularly young children and their mothers, need to be viewed as a continuum, whose lives are intertwined. The argument to include them in both the teams was, and continues to remain, strong.

A second dimension which has emerged is the need

to separately focus on adolescents and young people as part of our work. Presently, we are addressing the issues of school going children through our children's team and out-of-school adolescents through women's team. We are in process of developing a separate portfolio to address the concerns of adolescents and young people's health and nutrition.

CHETNA has consciously avoided opening field offices. We had ventured down that road when the evaluation by PRIA in 1990-91 clearly highlighted that in order to show impact, we had to concentrate our work in one or two states. We chose to work in the field in Gujarat and Rajasthan due to geographical proximity and our combined knowledge of the culture and language of the two states. The demand for our work in Rajasthan increased and we made a decision to open an office in Jaipur in 1997.

When a woman-led organisation was invited by the Government of Rajasthan to set up an office in the capital city, some local organisations became hostile. Resistance grew when we set up the field office with a woman in-charge. They resented the competition they perceived CHETNA to be, particularly since CHETNA has a formidable reputation of working without political connections. Majority of development organisations in Rajasthan are led by men, many of whom have family and political connections. Rajasthan is traditionally a feudal state and patriarchy is experienced at all levels. The bonding between male leaders of organisations and political leaders is so strong that it does not permit women to enter this fortress. Women are either worshipped and are to be kept at home or, if they enter the workforce and as leaders, they have to behave like men. Networking is normally done late in the evening when men meet after work, often over drinks. Government officers are invited to such meetings to advocate with them on issues. Generally women do not have the time or the interest (due to household and child care responsibilities) to attend such meetings and many perceive them to be unsafe. While there were some administrative issues, our inability to make a breakthrough in this male dominated work culture led to CHETNA closing its Jaipur office in 2005. The initiation and closure of CHETNA's office in Rajasthan has strengthened our belief that gender inequitable organisations produce gender inequitable results.

Currently, CHETNA has a broad, participatory decision-making model, though it has supervisory reporting/accountability mechanisms. We have standardised systems, though there still tends to be informality in processes. Each person's views, including that of new team members, are valued and taken into consideration. While the vision and mission guide the overall work of CHETNA, within each team, members are encouraged to innovate. The main aim of this form of organisational structure is to ensure each person is recognised and to promote collective ownership and accountability in a culture that gives space for innovation.

9

The art, science and isolation of leadership

It is well known that anyone who starts an organisation is always a strong leader with a definite philosophy and ideals which start getting more fixed with success and the positive growth of the company. The personality and style of the leader plays an important role in creating the DNA and behavioural style followed by all. I observed that Indu's thinking, her insights and her approach to issues and challenges are far superior and come very spontaneously from her. She led from the front. Indu always had a very forceful way of expressing and there was no grey areas in the way she communicated. Visionary and forward thinking was encouraged. This is often a key characteristic of successful people.

— Anu Wakhlu, Former Governing Council Member, CHETNA and Managing Director, Pragati Leadership Institute, Pune

One phrase that is commonly used to describe me is 'born leader'. "You have such a powerful personality that one cannot miss your presence in any place, event or meeting. You did not always sit in the middle during a team meeting in CHETNA, but it was always very apparent that it was you who was the leader," Dr Gahver Kapadia told me. Dr Kapadia was a senior member of the CHETNA team for eight years. This outsiders' image of me is puzzling to me, because as a child and young girl I was shy, retiring, preferring to stay in my room and read books, while the neighbourhood children played in the park or took part in the numerous activities my mother would think up.[6]

Does my positive, focused approach to undertaking and finishing tasks make me a 'born leader'? I have always been a doer, not content to simply have an idea and leave it at that. Sushmita Ghosh, Former President

---

6. Recently Sushmita Ghosh, President, Ashoka, shared an article with me, "Ten Reasons Why Introverts are Incredibly Attractive People" (*http://www.lifehack.org/articles/communication/10-reasons-why-introverts-are-incredibly-attractive-people-2.html*). When I read the article, it resonated with me, giving me a better perspective on how, though I grew up shy and almost a loner, I became an independent leader.

at Ashoka Headquarters in Arlington, says I am a serial doer.

> No sitting and ideating for Indu if she gets a whiff of an idea that just might be good. After a board meeting that we both attended, we discussed an idea on the car ride back. The minute she reached her office, a project named Children in Charge was floated, soon got funding, and became a nationwide project!

Innovative ideas, well implemented in the field, are innovations in CHETNA. As my organisational responsibilities grew, others may have undertaken the hands-on implementation, but I always follow through, paying attention to the process and the outcomes. I am open to ideas during the process, allowing decentralisation of decisions in the field, but the process is clearly my baby. Only when I am satisfied that the innovation is tried and tested, I let go. Not all innovations tried have succeeded at CHETNA. Failure only drives me to try again, till we get it right.

Any success is the result of the work of a team. Each team member is accountable for different tasks which are suitable to their personality and ability and I push them to work hard, to get maximum output.

> Indu is authentic...She stands for what she stands for, and will carry that everywhere she goes, infecting all around her. Always open to critique, her authenticity never translates into dogma. In fact, she continually turns to touchstones she trusts to validate, improves or discards her notions. Open but strong, determined yet flexible, Indu remains true to her goals even as she refines her strategy to achieve them. To ensure buy in, collective decision making, and a participatory and consultative approach to policy making and project implementation are now a part of the culture of CHETNA. At the same time, Indu is known to have sent back reports and proposals to their originators, overflowing in ample red corrections for shoddy quality! She has empathy at the core of all she does. Not power. Not achievement. Not ambition. But an intuitive understanding of what would be fundamentally helpful for her constituency. This makes her a trustworthy leader.
>
> — Sushmita Ghosh, Former President,
> Ashoka Headquarters, Arlington, US.

Indu catalyses connections, conversations and co-creation amongst diverse stakeholders to create breakthroughs in food security, gender equity and health for all," says Arun Wakhlu. "While this may appear to be a massive task, it is not so when we ride on the breeze of the 'creative intelligence' that runs all of life.

Creativity, for me, is important in leading an organisation. As a young person I used to sing. In college, I participated with enthusiasm in cultural festivals. I have kept alive my interest in aesthetics and performing arts and I believe this has contributed significantly in how I have shaped and led CHETNA.

My artistic interests have most vividly found expression in the physical spaces that we have created in which the CHETNA team works. In the initial years, I used my artistic abilities in creating posters, pamphlets and CHETNA's diverse educational aids. I was always conscious not to create art for art's sake; I wanted the design of CHETNA's educational material to take forward what we wanted to communicate. Which is why each CHETNA publication is extensively field tested with marginalised communities and the feedback received is critical in reworking the layout. "At CHETNA, I visualise artwork and design as communication, not merely as art. I have learnt the importance of gender for bringing a change in society and all my work (publications, posters, kits, etc.) communicates positive and gender balanced visuals and design," says Anil Gajjar, senior graphic artist at CHETNA, who joined the organisation in 1988.

When CHETNA got a separate office space, I took great interest in the interior design. I proposed floor seating, because this was the preferred option expressed by people coming from the field. They were usually uncomfortable sitting on chairs at formal tables in fancy conference rooms. I am proud of our Indian heritage, and used textiles and furniture from Gujarat and Rajasthan. My dreams and aspirations of creative spaces were fulfilled when CHETNA was generously offered three houses in the walled city of Ahmedabad for our work. These have become an ideal space for organising trainings and have served the purpose of residential spaces, especially for women, to encourage participation.

I strongly believe that design of the physical space influences organisational culture, and even gender sensitivity within organisations. In the 'parde ke peeche' rented premises which was our first office, we all sat on the same floor. When we needed more

Initiation of work at the Lilavati Lalbhai Bunglow (1991)

space, we occupied the second floor. In my experience, maximum work and synergy was achieved when we were sitting on the same floor.

In December 1992, we shifted to the beautiful Lilavati Lalbhai bungalow. The late Lilavatiben had willed that her bungalow be used by an organisation working on women and children's health but it was not to be used as a hospital. The trustees of her estate granted the premises to CHETNA on a long, rent-

free lease. We were housed here for 17 years. In that time, when we needed to expand, we were fortunate to be given two other properties on similar rent-free leases. Uniquely, all the properties were owned by women. CHETNA's Shahibaug office was located in the bungalow offered by Lilavati Lalbhai; CHETNA's office in the old city was housed in a bungalow owned by late Pratima Mehta; and CHETNA's Conference and Training Centre in the walled city of Ahmedabad was in a house owned by late Ms Meeraben Kirtidev Chinubhai. I remain forever indebted to the generosity of these three visionary women. I have greatly benefited and learned from my interactions with Pratimaben and Meeraben and though I never met Lilavatiben when she was alive, I am sure it would have been a privilege to interact with her too.

When the time came for us to move from the Lilavati Lalbhai bungalow, the Nehru Foundation for Development suggested we acquire land and build an office. But we realised that the land CHETNA could afford in the budget available was not suitable, as they were located in the outskirts of the city and women would have to travel great distances, spending an unreasonable amount of time to reach work. They would be anxious about the travel time, which would ultimately affect the quality of their work.

Eventually we chose to purchase an empty floor in a property adjoining the main bus terminus which I knew would be a convenient location not only for women but also for the male team members. In addition, the entire floor provided a great opportunity to design a work space for CHETNA which would reflect its values of transparency and openness. Spaces for team discussion for collective and participatory processes would be important components of the design.

We hired a feminist architect who designed the individual and team work spaces using only furniture. This has proved to be extremely facilitative in ensuring outputs, reflections and sharing among team members. In addition, we have a common dining space which encourages continuous informal interactions among teams. There are only three enclosed spaces in the entire office — the conference room and the cabins of the director and additional director (only for reasons of privacy as they would need to resolve conflict issues). The cabins have transparent glass doors and windows.

As the spaces are designated only by furniture, they are flexible and can be changed as per individual requirement. Unfortunately, the endless collection of paper and documents on individuals desks still bothers me; they have to be shifted too each time the space is reorganised!

I balance my compassionate, gender sensitive and creative side with my focus on tasks and performance. This is evidenced by appropriate systems for monitoring and review to ensure accountability. In place are regular audits of procedures and evaluation of the impact of our activities on women and men, and on gender relations.

I have led CHETNA intuitively, relying on my natural abilities and using my interests (artistic in particular) to further the principles I believe in. Perhaps that is what all leaders are born to do.

•

When CHETNA was set up, I doubted my ability to lead it, even going so far as to resist the designation of Director. Going to Boston in the autumn of 1988 to study at the Boston School of Public Health was a

Interaction on "Gender" with designers from National School of Design (NID) Ahmedabad, India

turning point in my leadership experiences.

It was my first trip to the USA and I was looking forward to studying and soaking in the diverse cultural and social experiences. Sharing an apartment with a young Spanish doctor from Barcelona was extremely educative. We instantly became friends.

While the three months I spent in Boston was a very enriching cultural experience, the content of the course itself was not very meaningful for me. I kept trying to link the theoretical course content to my lived reality of working in rural India. In every class I would continuously ask questions, seek clarifications. But these were usually left unanswered as the young teaching assistants who taught us were unable to provide the answers. I soon became the link for several Asian students between the theory we were learning and the practice based assignments we had to submit. Many assignments were completed with all of us huddled in our apartment, working through the night.

This contribution was recognised by the Boston School of Public Health when they offered me a position as a teaching assistant on finishing the course. If I had stayed back, I could have taken two more short courses and earned a degree in public health. I declined the attractive offer and returned to India.

While the course did not add much value to my lived knowledge and skills, I appreciate the huge learning experience it was. It brought home the fact I was adequately equipped to lead CHETNA and take the organisation's vision and mission forward in India and in other countries, particularly South Asia.

•

My leadership journey has been exciting and fulfilling. It has also been isolating, in a way. The task of taking the lead in ideating and creating, of building systems and processes, is rewarding, but it can be exhausting too. To be treated as the one who always has the answers is not always satisfying. Often there are times when as a leader I did not want to talk to anybody, to lead. Whom could I talk to, to express my doubts? To whom could I show my feet of clay?

The discontent of leadership is made bearable by finding fellow travellers, those who understand the distinctiveness of your path, yet treat you like an ordinary peer. I have been fortunate to have found such friends in my chosen field. During the 1980s, it was rare to see women in leadership positions and those who did were isolated from the strong clique of male leaders. In such a hostile environment, when I met several inspiring women leaders during my international travels, particularly to neighbouring countries in South Asia (which have a similar social structure), I naturally bonded with them. They shared their experiences of how they dealt with male patriarchy, of how they created spaces for themselves in such a patriarchal milieu and this greatly contributed to CHETNA's gradual evolution as a gender sensitive organisation.

One such courageous woman whom I bonded with was Late Perveen Rehman working in the Orangi Pilot project in Karachi, Pakistan. I first met her when I had gone to Pakistan to give a talk on young women's reproductive rights at the Aga Khan University, Karachi. On my way, I had slipped in the airport before boarding my flight, but was so excited to be visiting Pakistan for the first time (it had taken me three months to get a visa) that I did not feel the pain. At the end of the flight, my swollen foot made it difficult for me to walk. As soon as my hosts received me, they took me to a doctor who declared I had suffered a hairline fracture which required a plaster. I attended the conference in a wheel chair.

Perveen Rehman, who had come to attend the lecture, was extremely empathetic to my condition. She also offered to take me to meet her mother (originally from India) and sister before I left. When I reached the airport to travel back, all flights to India had been cancelled due to the aftermath of the riots on December 6th 1992. In spite of the influence of the Aga Khan Foundation, who had invited me to Karachi, I was unable to get a seat on a flight back to India for 10 days. During those 10 days I was an invalid, Indian guest, yet I have never been so well looked after in a foreign land. I made long-lasting friendships in that time. I got to know Perveen and the work of the Orangi Pilot Project. She volunteered to take care of me during my stay. She realised very quickly that I am a wanderer/gypsy who yearns for adventure, and in those 10 days, she would pick me up in a jeep (which she drove), take me to her office, her home, to visit friends, and even to bazaars for some shopping. She would wheel me around the bazaars/slum areas with gay abandon not bothered that I may be recognised as an Indian. The only caution she took was to ask me not wear a bindi and she changed my name.

What helped us bond was that we were in the same life stage — 30+ and single. My mother belonged to Lahore and hers to India. It was one of the best times of my life. The care, concern, fun and adventures did the work of painkillers.

Another peer who became an extremely good friend was Late Nasreen Huq. She was working as a nutritionist with BRAC (formerly Bangladesh Rural Advancement Committee). She also volunteered with Naripokko, a Bangladeshi feminist organisation. I first met her at BRAC when we had been invited to conduct a women and health workshop. Though Pallavi and I had gone completely prepared, we had not realised that apart from the leader and Nasreen, the rest of the senior male participants resisted our young leadership and doubted whether we would be able to deliver the outcomes. They expected us to start the training with statistics. But when we presented a gendered perspective, their egos were so hurt that they almost held a dharna[7] inside the training hall. The men had never experienced young women trainers and even though their leader was a woman, because she was raised in Bangladesh and was a medical doctor, they respected her. We were non-doctors (and young women at that) which made it very difficult for them to accept us as credible trainers on women's health.

---

7. Dharna: a protest.

We decided to take a short break. Nasreen, having a background in the women's movement in Bangladesh (she was the younger sister of Shireen Huq, a strong feminist leader in Bangladesh), took us aside to explain the background and socialisation of males in Bangladesh. Collectively we developed a strategy and managed to complete the assignment somewhat successfully.

I found a soul-mate in Nasreen that day. Even though we lived in different countries, we were professional nutritionists who wanted a world where both men and women lived and worked together to solve the issues of the marginalised sections of society. Our paths were destined to cross, I feel. I met Nasreen again in a meeting organised by ARROW to develop a Gender Sensitive Resource Kit. We shared a room. She was already on the ARROW Programme Advisory Committee; for me, it was my first meeting. Our friendship was grounded when we met regularly after I was selected to serve on ARROW's board.

Rashidah Abdullah and Di Surgey of ARROW, are other women with whom I share deep friendships as co-travellers. "Whilst our communication styles reflected very different cultural perspectives, our content and our motivations, our organisational experience and our aspirations were extraordinarily similar," says Di Surgey. "We each were passionate about women's health and wellbeing. We each were 'on' about gender sensitive, appropriate, accurate, useful, meaningful information being a tool for the engagement of otherwise disempowered women. We each understood, truly, the value of inclusion and participation not just in the building of an organisation

In a lighter moment with South Asian Leaders Dr Rashidah Abdullah, Founder Director ARROW Malaysia and Late Nasreen Huq (Naripokko, Bangladesh)

but also in the naming and sharing of women's truths. We recognised that we could learn from each other."

These soul-sisters have given me much sustenance and bolstered my courage to keep working and leading.

10

A workplace for women (and men)

> Besides the evident concern for indigenous traditions, preservation of local culture and co-creating sustainable futures, there are also other aspects of a gender sensitive and compassionate culture that you find in CHETNA: equal employment opportunities for men and women, a governing council with a balance between men and women, policies that reflect sensitivity to women's needs and commitment to gender equality at the programmatic level.
>
> — Arun Wakhlu, Former Governing Council Member, CHETNA and Executive Chairman, Pragati Leadership, Pune

On completing her MSc in Foods and Nutrition, Jyoti Gade was looking for a lecturer's job. She approached the home science department of a reputed arts college in Ahmedabad. There were no vacancies, but the college was helpful and showed her CHETNA's advertisement for 'field trainer' as her qualifications were appropriate for the role described. She applied for the post and was selected. When the college had a vacancy and they called her to apply, she politely declined, going so far as to thank them, because if it had not been for the advertisement they had shown her, she would not be doing what she loves — being in the field. The creative and interesting work, learning opportunities, and her personal and professional development kept her at CHETNA for 24 years.

Jyoti had wanted to pursue her PhD, but had given up the dream due to professional and personal commitments. It was through CHETNA that she got the opportunity to study for a Master's in Gender and Development in Netherlands. The course helped her broaden her vision on gender, gender inequalities and the role of gender in development.

Jyoti no longer works in CHETNA, and being on the outside she objectively says that CHETNA is a strongly gender sensitive organisation, because:

- Gender is integrated in the vision, mission, goals and objectives of the organisation.
- There is a clear mandate for a commitment to gender equality and gender mainstreaming.
- All the senior posts are held by women.
- There is an equal number of men and women on the governing council.
- There is regular monitoring and evaluation of the impact of its activities on women and men and on gender relations.
- Interventions in the field and organisational policies focus on women's practical needs and women are supported to define and meet their needs.
- The organisation offers equal employment opportunities for men and women.
- The organisation provides opportunities for all employees to equally participate in all activities.
- The organisation offers maternity and paternity leave.
- As required, a crèche facility is available for employees, even during trainings.

•

When I started CHETNA (and till this day), my intention was to do transformative work. In hindsight, I think the organisation was lucky that I did not come with the baggage of a management degree. It freed me from presumptions about gender-specific policies and what it takes to build an organisation, or specifically a gender sensitive one.

As CHETNA grew, we needed rules and procedures for all organisational aspects, including office timings, leave entitlements, travel, etc. I knew my personal preferences regarding office hours may not work for an organisation which mainly had women. I am a morning person and my 'office hours' practically begin at 5.00 a.m. Afternoons are usually reserved for meetings or discussions, and I like to be home by early evening. It was clearly not realistic to institute office timings that began at 6.00 am! After extensive discussions with all my women colleagues about their family responsibilities, we decided to start office work at 10.00 am. However, my body rhythm did not change and I continue to begin work early, at home, coming to the office by 10.00 am and leaving at 5.45 pm, when the office closes. It leaves me fairly exhausted, with limited time to pursue my other interests, but the women are happy and satisfied because they have the time to complete their family and household responsibilities before coming to work. Organising any after-office activities has always been challenging as they have to return on time to fulfil their never-ending household responsibilities. A few years ago, we introduced flexi timings with some common working hours to ensure collaborative teamwork.

The guidelines for pregnancy leave were instituted in 1984 as we recognised from the start that to deny this entitlement would be discriminatory. Paternity leave of two weeks was also introduced as another gender sensitive measure in 1998. Other generous leave provisions have also been introduced. We have built second and third line leadership so that gaps are not felt when some women require long leave, for example, during a difficult pregnancy. We optimise their time by finding some work that they can do from home. Every challenge is turned into an opportunity at CHETNA.

It is my belief that women come to the workplace to develop their potential. Through its organisational design and policies, CHETNA provides each and every individual, particularly women, with capacity building opportunities in their area of interest to develop their full potential.

Women by nature and to a great extent through socialisation are schooled to adjust to the needs of everyone around them. They also do not easily voice their opinion unless specifically asked. It is this observation and insight that led me to develop an organisational culture of participatory decision-making at all levels, where everyone's opinions are taken and recognised, particularly those of the quieter women. Often men take the credit for achievements while it is the women who work hard behind the scenes. In our documents, for example, we acknowledge all the contributors, the entire team, that has worked on a project, not just the author of the document.

Women are pivotal in the organisation. Their way of working with systematic planning and without gender bias is important for CHETNA to reach its goals. CHETNA has an equal opportunity hiring policy, but where competencies and qualifications are equal; we actively support the woman candidate. Throughout the history of CHETNA we have had women leaders in all departments (including administration and accounts). We have broken the stereotype — more men are employed in secretarial and assistant positions and more women in leadership positions. Our external consultants — designers, architects, auditors, documentation experts — have generally been highly qualified and competent women.

•

There is no doubt CHETNA is led by women, at all levels. We started with three women, and we have encouraged other women to join us in working on women's and children's issues. But this does not mean that we don't want men to be part of the organisation's journey.

Unfortunately, while men have been encouraged to join CHETNA, a majority of them have not stayed, particularly in senior positions. Some left because they found women's leadership a challenge and were not able to work under women, others because of greater career aspirations. In fact, it has been our experience that women workers are more comfortable reporting to women. Within the senior team too we are more comfortable being an all-women core group, as the presence of men often hinders open discussions.

For men, working with a team of women can be overwhelming. This was brought home to me when I asked Sanjay Joshi, a former CHETNA team member and now an independent consultant, what it was like for him as man to work in CHETNA. He joined CHETNA in 1987, entering the development sector for the first time.

Sanjay told me before coming to CHETNA he looked at the issues related to nutrition, maternal and child health, including child education, in an isolated manner. For example, a child with diarrhoea meant the child had ingested contaminated water, and hence the child was passing watery stools, resulting in dehydration and perhaps death by dehydration. Curative measures were needed to prevent dehydration and stop the diarrhoea. Now he had to start looking at the preventive measures too that needed to be taken for the future, such as sharing information on types of worms in green vegetables.

Women's perspectives and sensitivity to women's needs was new to him, especially because he grew up in a household with two brothers and no sister. He had never seen or experienced discrimination or disrespect of women at home. He studied in an all-boys convent school and his parents instilled an ethic for work both inside and outside the home. And then he arrived in CHETNA, where the talk and the walk were women-centric. As a man he often felt at a disadvantage!

> Travel to remote areas meant that lodging facilities would be bare," he told me. "The women from the team would capture the lone bed, or room, or bathroom. I would be pushed out — to sleep in the corridor or the veranda, and even on top of the jeep. Once in Banaskantha, being the only man, I was assigned a spacious room all to myself at the guest house, and the women team members had to crowd in to a small single room. They all declared me insensitive! All this was very confusing at one level. Why these women were behaving like women, I thought.

Writers and Editors of the launch of ARROW kit on Women-Centred and Gender-Sensitive Resource Kit (1996)

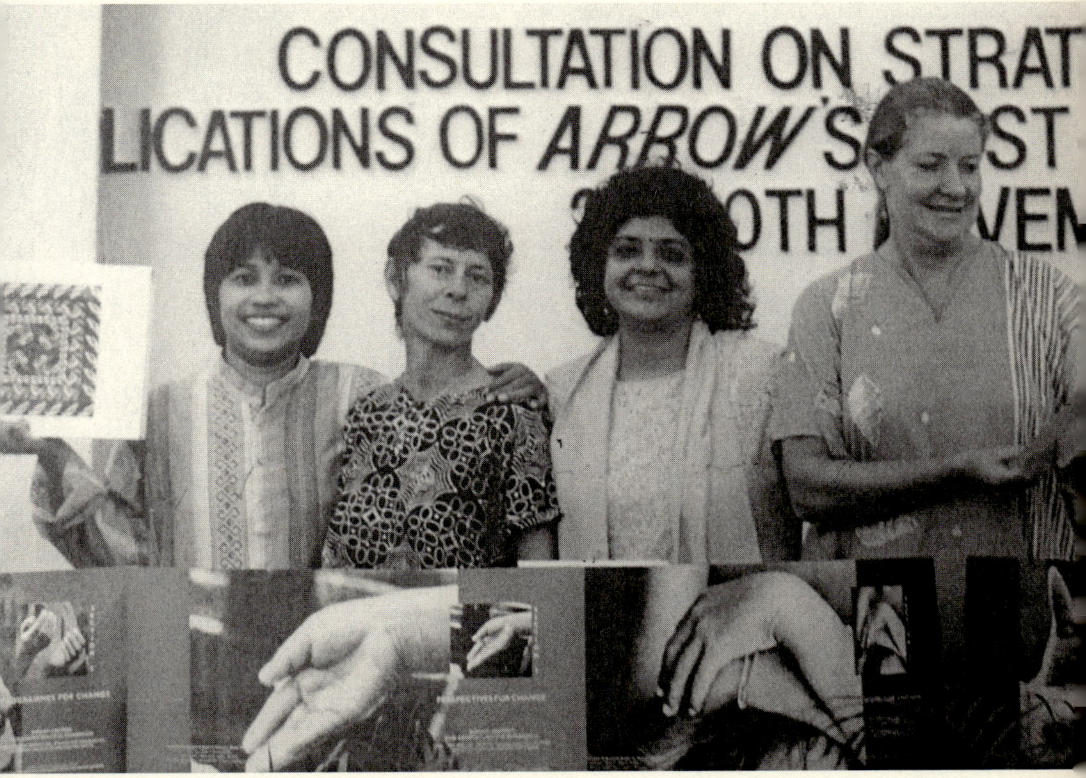
CONSULTATION ON STRAT
LICATIONS OF ARROW'S

With ARROW staff and Programme Advisory Committee (PAC) members (1996)

Having worked now for 30 odd years with women and young girls — be they poor, rich, literate, illiterate, farm labourer, housewife, weaver, or even a sex worker — I have realised that one has to have a bag full of compassion and empathy. At CHETNA I truly learnt to be a MAN — as envisaged by women — sensitive, caring, creative, concerned

> … To walk the talk, I needed far greater sensitivity and empathy as well as knowledge to help poor women, who are so strongly bound by cultural and social norms, to break free. Positive discrimination for women is necessary if women have to move forward. This will take time.

Sanjay's words reinforced to me that men and women negotiate the workplace differently, and if we have to build gender sensitive organisations, we need to be aware of these differences and not presume that what works for women would automatically work for men, and vice versa.

11

Partnerships for growth

CHETNA has always believed in collaboration with others for more effective impact. Since most communities are not homogenous and everyone has different needs, CHETNA's strategy has been to collaborate with individuals and institutions with different sets of skills and expertise and unite these diverse interests to address the needs of the marginalised.

Working with diverse partners to bring about change: Dr Sharada Jain, NGO partners (Former Director Sandhan and Doosra Dashak, Rajasthan) Dr Vivek Joshi (IAS) Government of India and Researcher (ICRW) (2013)

Partnerships with civil society

From the beginning, Pallavi, Minaxi, and I were clear that we wanted our interventions and innovative communications to reach the largest number. However, we made a choice not to do this by expanding our field presence, i.e., by creating subsidiary offices/branches all over the state. (Our expansion to Rajasthan was a great learning experience.) We wanted to remain a small team. We realised that this would limit the impact we made (diverse dialects and socio-cultural differences even within a state made it more difficult to widen our reach). Adopting such a strategy meant we had to find a way, find other like-minded people and organisations to help us increase the outreach of our work. We decided to identify field partners through

whom we would implement our interventions, and started looking for community based organisations working at the field level.

This proved easier said than done. There were a very limited number of field level organisations working on the issue of health and education at the time. Between those that existed there was (and still is) a large gap in perspectives and capacities. We did not want to set up new NGOs or community based organisations (CBOs) to build capacities of existing field organisations based on the philosophy we believed in. We made a small beginning, and slowly and steadily we were able to create a pool of local level organisations who have become CHETNA's partners. Without them, CHETNA would not have been able to achieve the impacts at the family and community levels that it has. Many of our partnerships have been instrumental in developing the pioneering health interventions CHETNA is recognised for today.

Inspiring a group of leaders from SHEHA, Mumbai, who work in urban slums

SEWA, Ahmedabad, has been a partner from the beginning. SEWA was working in the area of creating employment/livelihoods, and when they started a health programme, they approached CHETNA to train and build capacities of their health workers. "The team of Indu, Pallavi, Minaxi, Jyoti and Ila were young and energetic," remembers Mirai Chatterjee, Director, SEWA Social Security.

> We shared the same perspective on women's rights and gender equality. They were trained experts in nutrition, health and child development. It was

a natural fit for both of us. Over the years, we have joined hands with CHETNA on a number of occasions, in Gujarat and nationally, to push for gender-sensitive and appropriate health, nutrition and child development policies. Indu and I are on the Advisory Group for Community Action (AGCA) of the National Health Mission for several years. We have worked closely to integrate the ideas and experiences with our Shankarbhuvan sisters and others in community action for improved health and nutrition. We have struggled to get a rights perspective into health policies and programmes, including for the poorest of women and informal health workers like *dais* (traditional birth attendants). We have jointly worked to develop a Gujarat Dai Sangathan to give local women the visibility and recognition that is their due. We have also developed the Gujarat Shishu Sangh to place the issue of early childhood squarely on the development agenda.

CHETNA has built similar long-term partnerships with NGOs working in states other than Gujarat. We have contributed to the women's awareness and health programme of the Sadguru Water and Development Foundation (SWDF), who work in tribal areas of

International Advocacy for people centred policies (2002)

Gujarat, Rajasthan and Madhya Pradesh. We recently reconnected with SWDF to undertake a nutrition survey for them to understand the impact of their agriculture and livelihoods programmes on the health and nutrition of the communities, particularly women and children, they work with.

Another extremely supportive and facilitative partner was the International Council on Management of Population Programmes (ICOMP), Malaysia. Dr Jay Satia as its Director was aware of our work since 1984 when he worked in the Public Systems Group at the Indian Institute of Management (IIM), Ahmedabad. When he joined ICOMP, he invited CHETNA to several health leadership workshops, particularly on family planning, for South and South East Asia leaders. This led to CHETNA being invited as a technical resource to contribute a project aimed at developing and testing alternative approaches for adolescent sexual and reproductive health. On his return to India, Dr Satia has continued to collaborate with CHETNA through the prestigious Indian Institute of Public Health, Gandhinagar (IIPHG).

CHETNA's educational materials and training modules are in great demand in other states and at the national and international levels. Our expertise is sought in developing modules for trainers and materials for every cadre of health, education and nutrition frontline workers.

While it would have been easier and faster to create, employ and train our own health/link workers in the short run, in the long run it has been a much more sustainable strategy to build capacities of existing NGOs and community based workers who are familiar with the local dialect and have built relationships with the communities in field locations.

Partnerships with government

Since the 1980s, when CHETNA began its work, we have realised that while NGOs and community organisations undertake some excellent pilots, their work (and impact) remains limited due to the limited outreach of individual organisations. They also find it difficult to bring their work to the attention of government.

CHETNA's first foray in working with the government was to develop an educational kit on anaemia and women's health for the Directorate of Adult Education at the national level. Only a few copies of the kit we developed were printed at the end of the project. However, with the stroke of a policy maker's pen, we saw our creative work reach a much larger audience when the order was given to replicate the kit all over the country. We had a similar experience when developing educational materials under the Integrated Nutrition and Health Action Programme for the Government of Gujarat.

These experiences strengthened our belief that engagement with the government would go a long way in helping us achieve our mission and vision. Innovative programmes could be implemented on a much larger scale using the government's machinery, infrastructure and multiple frontline workers at the ground level. CHETNA decided to actively collaborate with government to expand the reach of its innovative solutions and made advocacy of its own work and those of similar organisations a part of its impact strategy.

In the 1980s, the reputation and influence of NGOs in Gujarat was tremendous. NGOs were actively consulted in every area of development (water harvesting, enterprises, livelihoods, health, etc). The challenge in CHETNA's interactions with government did not arise from lack of credibility in the impact of our work. It arose because government officials had little or no experience of dealing with urban, educated, professionally trained young women. NGO leaders in Gujarat, who were generally respected and their advice sought, were typically above 60, male and operating from the Gandhian principle of Swaraj. Every time my team and I entered the corridors of power in urban attire, we felt the suspicion rise. What was our motive? We could hear the wheels turning in their heads. The response of these officials was either one of indulgently listening to us, or not listening to us at all. The end result was the same: we were brushed off as inconsequential.

In the beginning, my age and gender was a considerable barrier in actively engaging with the government. My appearance was a great deterrent too and I tried my best to overcome this hurdle, first by always wearing saris to a government meeting and later adopting plain glasses. However, as time went by, due to the seriousness of the cause CHETNA espoused, I started getting invited to policy interactions. My assertive interventions in these meetings were on the basis of my field experiences based on regular travel to the most interior areas of the state. Government officials and bureaucrats were forced to confront the reality of what I was seeing and reporting. Slowly they began respecting what I said and taking serious note of my suggestions. My youth and gender began to fade into the background. But the battle continues. Every now and then there will be a new male officer who looks at me with great suspicion.

Soon my reputation and credibility grew and recognition through a Young Innovative Manager Award bestowed on me by the prestigious Indian Institute of Management (IIM), Ahmedabad, attracted publicity. While I am not a great believer in awards, recognition and publicity, I must admit that it has helped in increasing CHETNA's credibility, especially with the

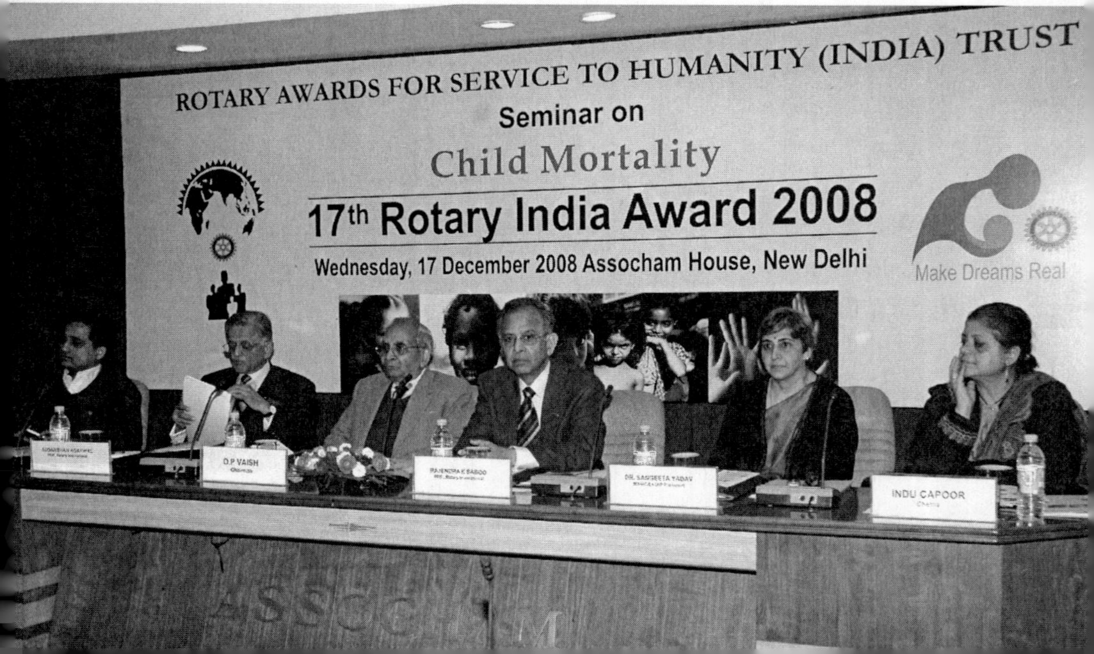

government. Since 2004, CHETNA has been recognised and financially supported by the Government of India as a Regional Resource Centre and Non-Government Nodal Support Organisation (NSO) in Gujarat in the area of health and nutrition. Our reputation and credibility is not restricted to the state level; we are one of the few health NGOs in India whose presence and advice is solicited in every important national consultation. This is no mean achievement as the leaders of other health NGOs are predominantly male and medical doctors.

Relationship with government is complex, as any NGO in the country will tell you. There are some who think we have been co-opted by the government, who blame us for remaining silent, especially during the Gujarat riots of 2002 when CHETNA was seen to be doing nothing. CHETNA has often challenged government decisions. When sex education was banned in Gujarat, we were at the forefront in pressurising the government to roll back its decision, giving them evidence from the ground on why sex education was critical for young people. It was in this period that CHETNA's book on adolescents, *Hum Tum* commissioned by the Government of Gujarat, was

Speaking at a Seminar on Child Mortality (Received Rotary Award for Service by Humanity India Trust) (2008)

widely discussed.

Our experience over three decades clearly suggests that an engagement strategy with the government has far-reaching effects in the longer term. It helps bring social sector views to the table, which is more likely to influence policy/programmatic change. Adversarial reactions can get us and the issue media attention and publicity in the short term, but does not necessarily influence policy or programmatic change. For civil society voices to be heard, we first need to be included and invited to policy discourse where we can place our arguments, armed with evidence from the ground. By engaging positively and bringing voices from the field, our opinions will be valued and integrated into

Advocacy with Ban Ki Moon (Secretary General of United Nations) at Mumbai

policy. There is no denying that this process is slow and it takes time to build credibility with the government, but in the long run it is a more sustainable strategy for change.

The proof that this strategy works is that over three decades, in spite of wide ranging political change at state and national levels, CHETNA's credibility and reputation with the government remains and we continue to remain relevant. We are consulted by the government on a regular basis on policy issues, our help is sought to upscale innovative programmes, and we have achieved the purpose of widespread acceptance of our training modules/materials. Engaging with the government has been one of the major factors why CHETNA has been able to reach out to all corners of the country and internationally.

Of media and religious leaders

The evening before CHETNA's board meeting in September 2015, I sat among the audience in a conference room in a hotel and watched Pallavi brief media persons on the impact of a recent project CHETNA was working on. There were newspaper and television journalists present, many of whom were not unfamiliar with CHETNA as an organisation or its work. Fifteen years ago, CHETNA would not have organised a media briefing. Interaction with the media and publicity was something I tried to avoid because I didn't want to engage with a media, which I saw as only interested in sensationalising an issue.

Looking back, I will say CHETNA's sojourn of working with the media began in 1992, when I became an ASHOKA Fellow.[1] After a decade of work on the ground and gaining some recognition at the state and national levels, I was looking to expand my horizons. I was fortunate to be shortlisted for an ASHOKA Innovators for the Public fellowship. I travelled to Kolkata to be personally interviewed by ASHOKA's founder, Bill Drayton. The experience was exhilarating as each question he asked helped me reflect on and understand myself and my actions. I received the fellowship in 1992 and was elected an ASHOKA associate member.

1. A/c Fellows are leading social entrepreneurs who are recognised as having innovative solutions to social problems and the potential to change patterns across society. See *https://www.ashoka.org/fellows*

As part of the fellowship, I requested ASHOKA that I would like to meet other ASHOKA fellows working in diverse fields. I met interesting practitioners in Bangladesh and Indonesia. In Thailand I met a young woman working with sex workers, which opened a new avenue of work for CHETNA in the area of HIV/AIDS education. In addition, I was invited to several fellow meetings. One of the earliest was at Ramakrishna Mission Ashram in Kolkata in 1992. In that meeting I was particularly impressed by the work of a conservation architect named Debashish Nayak. Little did I know then that we would be married in 1998.

As I began my CHETNA journey, I put marriage on the back burner. It's not that I purposefully decided not to get married, or that I didn't receive any proposals. I liked many of the men who proposed. But most of them expected me to give up my mission, give up building CHETNA, and shift to the city/town where they were located. This was unacceptable to me. I enjoyed my work, was busy building an organisation, and did not see why I had to be the one to sacrifice. Many people advised me that I would get lonely in later years, but

I was happy to remain single. Kartikeya was prescient when he told me not to worry; not only would CHETNA survive, he was sure the man I chose would happily move to Ahmedabad at the right time.

I was fascinated by Debashish's conservation work. CHETNA was housed in a heritage building and I invited him to come and see the CHETNA office building next time he was in Ahmedabad. Since he had been a student of architecture in Gujarat, he remembered the building (at the time called the Baitely Residence

and very famous among architecture students). He finally made a trip to Ahmedabad more than three years later (in 1996), and contacted me. That evening I was due to go for my friend's birthday party, and I invited Debashish to come along. At the party, a friend from Gandhinagar invited him to present his work to Mr Ghosh, then Secretary, Urban Affairs in the Gujarat government. Debashish readily agreed. One thing led to another and soon Debashish was appointed Advisor (Heritage) to Ahmedabad Municipal Corporation. He did not receive any compensation for this position. He did make a visit to Ahmedabad every month. Our friendship grew and we decided to marry. Debashish is a true democratic liberal; he believes every person needs to achieve his/her own potential. As he is fiercely independent himself, he understands everyone has the right to decide their own paths without harming anyone else. He did not once ask me to shift to Kolkata, as he felt that my work needed me to be in Ahmedabad while he could work from any city.

Today, Debashish and his work are well recognised in the city of Ahmedabad. He has contributed significantly in getting Ahmedabad's heritage recognised at the

Marriage at 40! (1998) Celebrations with close friends, long time CHETNA colleagues (Ila Vakharia and Jyoti Gade over 25 years)

national and international levels (through UNESCO's nomination as a World Heritage City). He has also contributed to the creation of the first heritage cell in Ahmedabad Municipality and is the First-Director of Centre for Heritage Management at Ahmedabad University.

In building what he calls a 'movement' for heritage, Debashish has not shied away from engaging with all stakeholders. He believes that those who are like-minded need to work with those who are 'un-like minded'. By not engaging with them, our work is not fully grounded and we limit the impact of the change we seek to bring. He has always been comfortable working with religious leaders and the media to build support for his cause.

I, on the other hand, used to be wary of politics, politicians, religious leaders and the media. But seeing the impact of Debashish's work, of getting recognition for heritage in the cities of Gujarat in a short span of 15 years, I opened my mind to engaging with the 'un-like minded'. Having seen first-hand how political commitment at the highest level can drive policy

implementation, CHETNA engages with politicians too, putting forward our views to them on the issues we work on. Such political engagement by CHETNA has borne fruit, particularly in driving the implementation of the Pre Natal Diagnostic Techniques (Prohibition of Sex Selection) Act (PCPNDT) which has impacted the sex ratio in Gujarat.

•

Working with the government and Members of Legislative Assembly (MLA's) works!

To build and gain respect in the long term, one needs to be focused, patient and persevering. The journey of a young, urban, educated woman who set up an NGO in the 1980s has been a long one. Apart from sincerity, commitment and focused results, the partnerships, networks and alliances that CHETNA has worked with in the past and will continue to build in the future has been a key aspect in achieving this success. CHETNA has been effective because in every issue that we work on we partner with multiple stakeholders at the policy and programmatic level.

Real partnership does not guarantee that the output of the effort will be in the desired direction that you may have visualised. But 'controlling' the outcome and micro-managing the direction of the inputs is contradictory to the principles of partnership. Today, many funding agencies, governments and corporate use the word partnership, but in reality they are looking for organisations to implement their vision, not build a common vision. Often some money (small grants) is given to ostensibly implement a project as conceptualised by an NGO, but the limited budgets, project duration and restricted timelines often do not allow the NGO to build relationships with the community or with the funding agency. Is it really possible to reduce malnutrition in poor and marginalised communities within one year?

Many funding agencies come with specific technical packages that sometimes do not have any leverage/ autonomy for changing the field implementation plan. They give sector wide funding which does not allow for comprehensive/holistic planning and implementation. In the name of Corporate Social Responsibility (CSR),

Launching the March to the Taj as the co-chairperson on White Ribbon Alliance of India (WRAI) with Shabana Azmi (2001)

several corporate organisations are adopting a similar approach to working with NGOs. This may result in some limited indicators being achieved, but not long term outcomes. Specialisation often leads to a tunnel vision, not sustainable solutions.

CHETNA's strategy of partnership is one where both (and all) partners collectively discuss the pros and cons of a strategy before it is adopted and where field action is planned in consultation with the community. This is not easy, given the environment and conditions under which funding is made available. It is getting more difficult to negotiate an equal partnership as some donors want to complete the entire project cycle in one year. In CSR, companies tend to compare their experience of implementing commercial projects with a project addressing social causes. Many assume that all NGOs have no professional training to implement projects cost effectively and therefore the corporate organisations have the right to dictate the terms of the relationship.

A partnership is not for a specific project, to be undertaken in a short period of time for a specific purpose. Partnership is a long term investment where the needs and concerns of each partner have to be respected and valued. In a predominantly patriarchal society where power is centred on one person without considering the needs and aspirations of others, unequal relationships are often the norm and this affects the growth and development of the entire society. How can we build an inclusive and equitable society if the needs and concerns of large sections remain unaddressed? To ensure sustainable development, we need to equally value the aspirations of all and this can be achieved by ensuring true partnerships at all levels.

12

Resourcing CHETNA

My work in interior, rural Gujarat in the 1980s was an enlightening experience. Travelling to some of the remotest villages of the state, I soon realised that all the resources we had was a mere drop in the ocean. Finding resources to sustain CHETNA's work was going to be an uphill and ongoing challenge.

When the demand for our training, education and materials grew, we started attracting funds. Initially it was for small projects. The first 'core grant' that we received was from Ford Foundation in 1984 for which we had to write a concept note followed by a larger proposal. Though the grant was not very large, it did enable us to rent separate office space and employ a 10 person team.

Looking back, it was a very flexible grant. We were not expected to develop detailed log frames or to give monthly, quarterly and six monthly reports. We gave a brief report every year. The direction of the project was not controlled by the donor but based on the needs that arose from the field. In fact, two years into the child survival project (as Ford Foundation called the grant), we realised that child survival was not possible without women's empowerment. We discussed this with the programme officer who was in charge of the grant and made changes in the project design. This seems impossible to do today as grants are given for a definite purpose for a specific, short period which hinders the achievement of a long term vision. Ford Foundation continued to fund us for nearly two decades, after which we received an endowment grant from them.

I feel very strongly that the flexibility of the grant and sensitivity of the Ford Foundation officer was instrumental in establishing and developing CHETNA. In fact, the Ford Foundation grant enabled CHETNA to evolve as it worked, as the donor did not stifle our aspirations or divert us from our vision and mission. If we want organisations in the social sector to grow and develop and serve community needs, donors should be facilitators and not force targets or outcomes, as this compels leaders to become short-sighted in their decision-making, which in the long term is actually harmful to the sustainability of an organisation.

Following the funding received from Ford Foundation, we received a grant from the Aga Khan Foundation (AKF) to implement the Child-to-Child programme in 1985. This grant took less time to negotiate as the reputation of receiving a grant from Ford Foundation helped negotiations with the new donor. AKF was interested in educational pedagogy issues and their outcomes. There was a separate monitoring agency which regularly measured the outcomes at the field level. The Programme Officer (Education) from the Geneva AKF office, Dr Ward Heneveld (himself an eminent educationist), took keen interest in the project and regularly monitored the direction of the grant in consultation with the programme officers who anchored the project at the AKF office in Delhi.

Dr Judith Evans, Programme Officer, AKF Geneva also took a keen interest and often asked pertinent

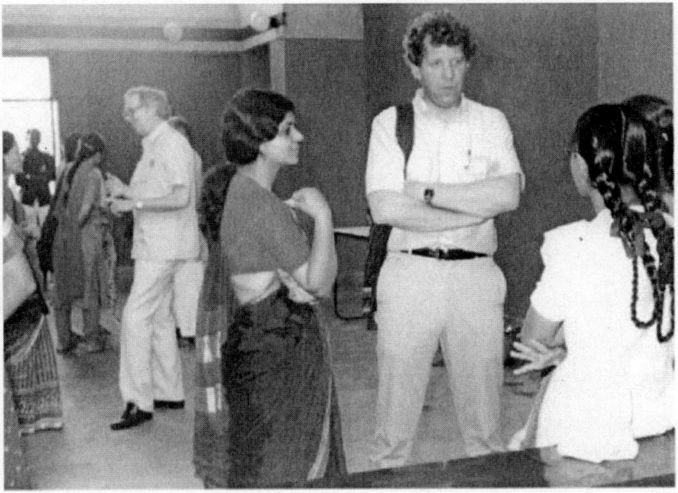

questions which forced us to reflect and re-think our strategies. Her expertise and interest was Early Childhood Care and Education (ECCE) and we learnt a great deal from her. AKF also sponsored several visits of the CHETNA team to conferences and seminars. In addition, the CHETNA team was exposed to building capacity of AKF partners in other countries (Sri Lanka, Kenya, Nepal and Bangladesh). In fact, AKF was instrumental in the initiation of the Child

Promoting the Child-to-Child Concept in India with Prof Hugh Hawes and Dr Ward Henevald (Fomerly Aga Khan Foundation) (1985)

Resource Centre at CHETNA along with Bernard van Leer Foundation, Netherlands. AKF's contribution to building CHETNA's own capacities is immeasurable. Although the relationship with AKF ended after six years (i.e., two grant cycles) as is their policy, we continue our relationship with all AKF staff, even after they have moved on to other responsibilities.

"During AKF's involvement with CHETNA, the organisation grew synergistically as new issues were identified and additional funding agencies were brought to the table," recalls Dr Judith Evans. "While expanding, CHETNA has remained true to its values, promoting women's leadership, beginning with empowering the woman herself, and then developing her leadership within her own family and the wider community".

Another facilitative and nurturing donor has been the BvLF. Their programme officer in India was Liana Gertsch, who had worked and lived in India and understood and empathised with the needs of Indian communities, particularly children. BvLF's initial funding was a small grant for translation of a children's book into local languages (Hindi and Gujarati) followed

by a grant to team leaders of the Child Resource Centre to attend the UN PrepCom in support of our advocacy work on child rights.

Our deepening capacities and credibility resulted in CHETNA being invited by different donors to build capacities of other NGOs across the county. The Ford Foundation grant continued. Based on our experiences in the field, where we were slowly learning about the impact of gender in development, especially on

Promoting Child Rights at a National Conference (2008)

Critical funders responsible for CHETNA's growth in early years (Ford Foundation 1984-2002 and John D. and Catherine T. MacArthur Foundation since 2002-till date)

women and girls, we started a separate Women's Health and Development Resource Centre (WHDRC) to work on health issues confronting women and girls, in particular their reproductive and sexual health and rights. This was funded by a grant received from the John D. and Catherine T. MacArthur Foundation in 1999 facilitated by its Regional Director, Poonam Muttreja. I had met Poonam when she was heading the fellowship programme in Shruti, an organisation based in Delhi. Though it was a brief meeting, she had left quite an impression on me because in spite of being a young woman she had held her own with all the senior mentors (read men) in Shruti. The MacArthur Foundation trusted us because of our track record and, similar to the Ford Foundation, further facilitated capacity building within CHETNA.

Our experience with donors has been mixed. Over the course of three decades, CHETNA has also worked on projects based on short-term grants (e.g., the growth monitoring training in difficult tribal areas of Panchmahals, Gujarat and Chandrapur, Maharashtra funded by USAID). While such projects reimburse human resources and travel costs, they have not contributed much to the long term vision of the organisation nor built capacities of the team. Seeking a solution within a limited area over a short period does not consider the problem holistically. Short-term resourcing (including human) is never sufficient for the committed work we do, and it often leads to frustration among the teams because a number of outputs have to be produced in a short period of time.

CHETNA has also observed that many donors use small grants to sub-contract their field work requirements. Once the field work is complete, the donor uses it for documentation and advocacy to increase visibility for themselves. In some instances, we have seen donors work at cross purposes in the same field area, which defeats the purpose of such interventions and certainly does not serve the local community. A few donors are known to question every expense incurred by field staff, while their national and international teams draw far larger salaries. Overheads, administrative and staffing costs of such donors far exceed the amounts they give to local NGOs/field staff. Such relationships are neither equitable nor fair.

•

Speaking on Nutrition and Food Security at the United Nations (2014)

There appears to be both a shortage and a glut of resources for NGOs today. Budget cuts from the current government for programmes related to women and children have significantly reduced resources available at the local level. Fund raising by NGOs within the country received a boost when business houses and Public Support Units (PSUs) were mandated under the

Companies Act, 2012 to contribute 2 per cent of their profits to the social sector. Unfortunately, this route is riddled with potholes involving advertising agencies demanding high fees and 'service charges' to facilitate contacts with their CSR counterparts in business houses. India has emerged as a 'donor' to many countries in Africa and Asia. Our gross domestic product (GDP) growth rate, pegged at 7 per cent compared to 0 to 3 per cent in many developed nations, discourages them from channelling funds through their respective development agencies. This has resulted in shrinkage of budgets of many NGOs, leading to curtailment of several pilot and innovative projects. At the same time, private foundations and philanthropy have begun to show interest in funding local innovations and social entrepreneurs are committing themselves to finding grass roots solutions to global problems.

Donors and development organisations can really make a great difference if a mutually beneficial partnership exists. This requires grantors to be sensitive to the needs and vision of the NGO and equally for the NGO to be committed and trustworthy. It is important that donors consider building the capacity of the organisation in the long term rather than fund projects with short-term outcomes. At a retreat facilitated by Dr Usha Jumani in 2005, CHETNA collectively developed criteria for accepting projects and we choose projects and find resources where there is scope and grants for capacity building, both of the staff and the organisation. This is not easy, but the spirit with which I began CHETNA — engendering society through nutrition and health interventions — holds us in good stead.

13

Governance in organisations

At the first governing council meeting that I attended in CHETNA, Minaxi Shukla, Additional Director, got up to make her presentation. "What I wish to say can best be expressed through a song, so please allow me to sing a small stanza," she requested. And she sang *Aa chalke tujhe main leke chaloon ek aise dagar ke taley/ jahan gham bhi na ho aansoo bhi na ho/bas pyar hi pyar paley* (Let me take you on a path where there is no sadness, where there are no tears and only love prevails). The sincerity, the innocence and the hope in her voice touched a deep chord in me and I found tears streaming down my face. In that moment I knew that my experience with CHETNA was going to be different from the numerous other boards I was on. From the aesthetics of jasmine flowers in small *katoris* made of dried leaves placed

> by the side of the cloth file with the agenda papers, to the home cooked delicious vegetarian lunch, the entire experience of board meetings at CHETNA is stripped of its stifling formalities and is an event I look forward to attending.
>
> I believe women are different from men — not better, not worse, but different — and that difference needs to be celebrated. CHETNA exemplifies that the female gaze must inform the way we look at all issues and find solutions to problems. That the human condition needs to be factored in, that the reality of women's lack of decision-making is what needs to change if our efforts have to bear fruit.
>
> When women are empowered they transform the very notion of power itself so it becomes about sharing and not about the powerful exercising dominance over the weak. CHETNA, and Indu Capoor as its leader, embodies this world view and therein lies hope...
>
> — Shabana Azmi, Activist, actor and
> CHETNA Governing Council member

•

Being one of the few women leaders in the 1980s, I was invited by many NGOs and CBOs to join their governing boards and management trustee councils.

My presence though seemed 'ornamental', often times fulfilling a requirement demanded by funding agencies. To add to the already existing bias against women, my youth and inexperience also worked against me. For the first few meetings, I was taken for granted. When I started raising issues, my suggestions were met with resistance. Soon I realised that in such governing boards, decisions had already been taken between the secretary and the managing trustee, and external board members were invited to fulfil a formality. Some board meetings finished in 45 minutes interspersed with a lot of food and occasionally alcohol (a pattern that is often typical of men-led organisations). There was a lot of male bonding and camaraderie, as many members were on each others' governing boards.

The one enriching experience I had was as a board member of ARROW and that is what I aspired for when I decided to set up a governing council for CHETNA. The need for a formal structure of external governance was resisted within CHETNA and the Nehru Foundation for Development (NFD) under whose aegis we existed. All major decisions related to finance and administration was being taken in consultation with the managing

Governance matters: Two gender sensitive chairperson's Dr Sharada Jain and Mr A.R. Nanda

trustee of NFD, Kartikeya Sarabhai. Why then was I insisting on a separate governing council for CHETNA?

From the inception of CHETNA I have believed in sharing our learning's from the field and I also believe that CHETNA needs to be independently accountable and transparent to all our stakeholders. It was one of the reasons for initiating our newsletter, *CHETNA News*, which was published in three languages (English,

Hindi and Gujarati) and widely distributed for 24 years. As we grew in size, handling multiple projects for multiple funding agencies, it became important to me that community needs external stakeholders help to guide our work, because often we are too close to a problem and cannot see the forest for the trees.

It would have been natural to ask the trustees of NFD to select the members of CHETNA's governing council. But in the participatory spirit and culture of CHETNA, the organisation's senior team members recommended a list of names which was finalised by the Trustees of NFD. We began by listing eminent people who worked on or were committed to the same issues as us from across the states in which CHETNA had worked. The idea of having governing members from different fields was welcomed by the NFD trustees. The list was circulated and each senior team member communicated their choice based on whom they considered the most appropriate. Each governing council member since then has been selected on 'merit' and not political or family connections. This not only makes it easier to interact with them, but I am sure they also feel valued.

I was very keen that a woman lead the council and we zeroed in on Dr Sharada Jain, an eminent educationist from Rajasthan whose wisdom and insights on numerous occasions had impressed me. Her first formal introduction to CHETNA was in 2002 when she was invited for a consultative meeting to evolve acceptable criteria for deciding 'seniority' and 'promotion' of faculty members. "That four-hour long interaction with Indu Capoor, Kartikeya Sarabhai, Minaxi Shukla, Pallavi Patel and others gave me a clear realisation that here is an 'organisation with a difference' — full of positive energy and daring. It was, therefore, a matter of great joy for me to receive an invitation from Late Mrinalini Sarabhai to join CHETNA as chairperson of its governing council. I accepted the offer as a matter of privilege," recounts Dr Sharada Jain.

CHETNA held its first governing council meeting on 12 February 2002. I vividly remember Ajay Mehta, Managing Trustee of SEWA Mandir, Udaipur, remarking that it was the most enriching governing council meeting that he had ever attended. In his experience, council meetings were boring, stiff affairs, held mainly to ratify what the trustees had already decided. At CHETNA, senior team members are invited and encouraged to present their work and achievements to the governing council and seek critical comments, suggestions and meaningful insights from the members. Each suggestion is taken seriously and this has helped us strengthen our strategy to achieve CHETNA's mission and vision.

Each member of the carefully selected governing council has always been truly participatory, contributing meaningful insights. Generally leaders/Chief Executive Officers seem anxious when preparing for their board meetings but I looked forward to them, because I saw them as learning experiences. Listening to enlightened critical analysis of CHETNA's work helped me refine the direction we wanted to take CHETNA in.

Usually the governing council is expected to raise funds, contact influential individuals and raise the organisation's visibility. However, in CHETNA, it is the senior team which approaches donors and raises resources. The governing council members serve as a brainstorming body which helps us see the larger picture and guide us in developing the future strategy of CHETNA. The Chairs of CHETNA's governing council have each been excellent facilitators raising crucial concerns related to our work and challenging our assumptions while greatly appreciating and supporting our endeavours. This is not to say there have not been any 'awkward moments', but all issues have been amicably resolved in the spirit of participation and consensus.

There has been some political interference in the choice of governing council members. Several government officers have sent me or Kartikeya feelers that they wanted to be nominated to the governing council. We have never considered such requests. At one point we were asked to by a powerful male politician of Gujarat to remove Shabana Azmi from our board. We did not oblige, telling him we would consider the possibility of replacing her on the board only when we felt Shabana was not making a meaningful contribution. The one or two people from the corporate sector whom we had on the council did contribute significantly but they resigned because they felt that the meetings focused too much on 'process' and not enough on 'impact'.

Essentially, CHETNA has been effective because its governance is participatory. A board is extremely important in the governance of an organisation but it should not be the source of top-down, centralised decisions. Decision-making should be the prerogative of the teams that are actually working in the field on the projects. Governing members who listen and support these decisions by guiding and mentoring the teams, providing vision, direction and wisdom, truly enable an organisation to grow.

14

Organisations need mentors too!

Mentoring is an increasingly popular way of providing guidance and support to young people in organisations to help them achieve career and personal goals. It helps grow talent, retain high-potential talent, and accelerate leadership development and readiness. It can also serve a strategic purpose when linked to talent strategy, leadership development, workforce planning and organisational goals.

We tend to associate mentoring with individual employees within an organisation or institution. In my opinion, the strategic purpose of mentoring, i.e., of helping individuals reach their goals and potential, applies just as well for organisations. CHETNA's professional and organisational growth would not have been possible without the support and guidance of many individuals and organisations. Several of them have facilitated CHETNA's journey of self-discovery and development by sponsoring us for courses, workshops and seminars, nationally and internationally. In essence, they have all provided mentorship to a fledgling organisation.

CHETNA was born when Ford Foundation agreed to fund a small project. Representatives of our initial core funding agencies not only gave us the seed core funding for CHETNA's foundation but also supported me and the team for our personal and professional growth. The trust Ford Foundation and Dr Saroj Pachauri in particular placed in me continued for 20 years and was reflected in an endowment grant being given to CHETNA by them in the year 2002.

"As a Programme Officer of the Ford Foundation, I made a grant to CHETNA which enabled Indu to start the programme," remembers Dr Saroj Pachauri. "I must confess, however, that making this grant to seed an organisation that would be managed by this girl who was just out of university (having qualified as a nutritionist) was somewhat unnerving at the time! What if Indu decides to get married and leaves the programme unfinished? What if she doesn't have the capacity to develop and organise the programme? These questions gave me some sleepless nights….

"Indu, however, took on the programme with great confidence, enthusiasm, and vigour. It soon became clear that she was in earnest and my fears were unfounded. I realised that Indu's ambitions were limitless. She wanted to extend programme coverage, but more importantly, she wanted to make a difference at the national level. Ford Foundation remained CHETNA's key donor for 20 years. But I encouraged Indu to diversify CHETNA's funding base. She responded by raising more funds from more donors."

Saroj is the most nurturing person that I have had the pleasure of knowing. A highly qualified and well respected professional, she is modest, charming and supportive to boot. She has served on CHETNA's governing council and remains my role model of funding agency representatives, which I constantly look for in future funding agencies.

Dr Meera Chatterjee working with United States Agency for International Development (USAID) fulfilled my expectations of partnerships with funding agencies. In continuation of our first grant, she asked if we could assist USAID in a growth monitoring project in Chandrapur (Maharashtra) and Panchamahals (Gujarat). I accepted the challenge as we were low on grants. We had two Marathi speaking trainers, Jyoti Gade and Ila Vakharia. It meant travelling in difficult districts where we had no office base. Hiring vehicles, equipment and local field workers also demanded a lot of time and resources. However, what made it worthwhile was the facilitation by Dr Chatterjee. Being a fellow nutritionist she also contributed to project design but always kept an open mind to learning's from the field. When she moved to The World Bank, she helped us organise 'development fairs', where we brought together NGOs and community based organisations to showcase their work and conducted daily seminars on development topics

Dr Meera Chatterjee first heard of me through late Dr Kamla Chowdhary with whom she was working at Ford Foundation. Their brief was to develop NGOs working in the field of nutrition. As a management expert Kamla was interested in building the organisation, whereas Dr Chatterjee's interest at the time was more in the subjects on which CHETNA's mission was focused — nutrition and health, women and children.

"I have had the good fortune of working with CHETNA on five very different 'projects' in the 1980s and 1990s," recalls Dr Chatterjee. "In 1986 we began a communications and training programme in the Government of India's ICDS (Integrated Child Development Services) Scheme in Panchmahals, a large tribal district of Gujarat, which was at that time being assisted by USAID. Gender differences in nutrition were already being reported widely, but a peculiar contradiction was emerging. While large-scale data for India and its states (particularly from the National Nutrition Monitoring Bureau which assessed ten major states) showed that, among children under five years of age, boys were more undernourished than girls, smaller studies by NGOs were revealing the opposite. During my work with CHETNA and other partners we sought to understand this contradiction. The work entailed extensive field visits to carry out formative research for communications and training efforts. The resolution of the gender conundrum of course lay in the question: Who is assessed? Clearly, because large scale data gathering is just that, families tended to bring out their 'prized' children — sons — and not their undernourished daughters, while smaller 'action' programmes that sought to deliver improvement services encountered girls as well. The programme CHETNA developed focused on improving the awareness of ICDS Anganwadi workers and mothers of the causes and management of malnutrition among children of both sexes. It included a focus on pregnant and lactating women because of the widespread prevalence of low birth weight which created a considerable handicap among children in addition to undermining child and maternal survival. The CHETNA effort with its focus on girls and women was a pioneering one."

Dr Chatterjee's second involvement with CHETNA was more focused on its institutional needs. My team and I were interested in developing capabilities for research and documentation, and requested Dr Chatterjee to help us. She designed and carried out DRAW — Documentation, Research and Writing — Workshops, involving about 12-15 CHETNA staff.

"It was through this process that I recognised that CHETNA was involving men too in its work," says Dr Chatterjee, "and that its nutrition and health, and women and child foci were not the exclusive preserve of women! This, too, was relatively unusual at the time, particularly in organisations headed by women. Of course, the majority of health-focused NGOs were headed by men! I believe that an important feature of Indu's leadership of CHETNA has been to bring a gender balance to her staffing."

Dr Chatterjee work with CHETNA eventually involved the production of a seminal report entitled *Learning for Life based*, among other resources, on a three-day workshop with significant people in the field. *Learning for Life*, based on the Child-to-Child approach, discusses the scope of communication, its methods and the great potential of children of both sexes communicating with each other and with parents (of both sexes) and communities.

CHETNA's Women and Health (WAH!) programme that began in 1988 was based on the life-cycle approach that Dr Chatterjee had advocated for in a report for the Government of India entitled *Indian*

Women: From Birth to Twenty. She was involved in CHETNA's initiating workshop and thrust, and subsequently moved on to advocate the approach more widely and work with the World Bank's projects and research on women's health. Erika Fink from the German Foundation for Development co-created WAH!

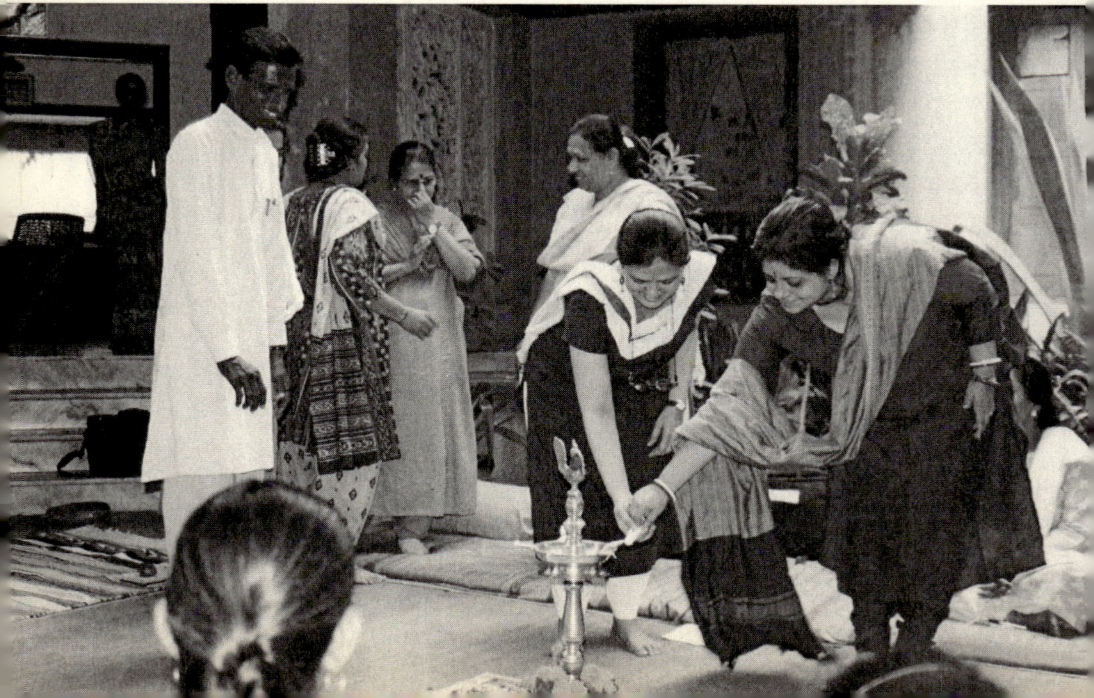

with a task force anchored at CHETNA, which till date forms the core for our understanding in addressing women's health in India from a comprehensive and gender sensitive lens. "There is no more important programme to address gender equity than one that focuses on women's health," says Dr Chatterjee. "It is at the heart of women's physical, psychological, mental, social and economic development, and also of the development of these aspects in children and families, and thereby in communities and the nation. Over the three decades that I have known CHETNA, its growth and development as an institution has been accompanied by an almost-unique versatility, an ability to absorb the latest thinking and trends and to develop its programmes accordingly. But in doing so it has not just served 'the need of the hour', or of the government (a significant client), or of donors, but it has focused on the real needs of people of both sexes, and particularly the poor and disadvantaged," Dr Chatterjee concludes.

The Aga Khan Foundation (AKF) who supported CHETNA for six years were wonderful and associating with Dr Sheila Vir and Rajni Khanna was an enriching experience. Sheila continues to take immense interest

Launching the Women and Health (WAH!). Lighting a lamp for empowerment and enlightment (1992)

in CHETNA's work. She vividly recalls her first visit to the CHETNA office. "Dr Ward Heneveld, who was then the programme officer in-charge of education portfolio at AKF at the Geneva headquarters, introduced me to the young, enthusiastic team at CHETNA. The organisation was one of AKF's major 'grantees'. I noted with interest that CHETNA had a team of women employees led by three women (Indu, Minaxi and Pallavi) who appeared extremely enthusiastic and passionate to undertake challenging tasks and improve the situation of women, adolescents and children in India. The fact that the organisation was fully managed by women at every level impressed me and did leave a lasting impression. The office was traditionally furnished and we comfortably squatted and discussed a wide range of development issues. Our dialogue was primarily concentrated towards finalising a project plan of action for experimenting with 'Child-to-Child' strategy in rural India. I continued to associate with CHETNA after moving on to UNICEF, India in New Delhi and continue to be impressed by the number of activities CHETNA undertakes to put women and their health, nutrition and empowerment central to the social development agenda of the country."

Dr Judith Evans and Dr Ward Heneveld truly cared about children and education. The CHETNA team and I have learnt from them how to implement educational projects for very young people and how to write winning project proposals. While they deeply cared about and were keen on outcomes and measurement, they were also very sensitive about processes and people development and travelled along with us to interior areas. Later, Dr Ward Heneveld joined the World Bank in Washington where he focused on education in Africa. He was also the Director of Society for International Development (SID) from where interns are sent to voluntary agencies. Dr Judith Evans is a recognised international expert on child development issues. CHETNA has actively kept in touch with both of them through their different avatars.

The AKF put CHETNA in touch with late Professor Hugh Hawes, co-founder of Child-to-Child Trust, UK. This inspiring partnership lasted for more than a decade. From the beginning CHETNA believed in children and their tremendous potential to contribute to the health and well-being of themselves, their families and communities. However, our ideas found roots when we came across the rights based approach to children's participation in health promotion and development initiated by Dr David Morley and Prof Hawes. Prof Hawes has been a great inspiration and guide who has helped CHETNA strengthen its belief in children and their abilities.

Prof Hawes visited CHETNA in 1985 and supported us in organising a Child-to-Child workshop, a pioneering and important milestone in the history of Child-to-Child in India. Since then, our learning has continued. Our association with the Child-to-Child Trust, particularly Prof Hawes, provided opportunities to take the approach not only into various parts of India but also to other countries like Kenya, Bangladesh, Sri Lanka and Thailand, where we have co-facilitated several Child-to-Child workshops with Prof Hawes and supported academic and community organisations to implement this approach.

Most government led programmes follow a top-down vertical model for delivering interventions. For example, the health sector focuses its various programmes on disease prevention and treatment and the education sector focuses on teaching subjects like social sciences, languages, maths and science. An enabling environment is a pre-requisite for child participation. Child participation cannot be implemented in isolation. It needs active support from adults, teachers and parents. Experiences and evaluations indicate that without sensitising adults, children can make limited changes. In India, children are viewed merely as recipients of the services that they need to survive, grow and develop. Adults around them (parents, teachers, health workers) are the providers or protectors of children. So children are expected to listen, take and follow instructions and obey orders. Children's own potential is rarely acknowledged and utilised in development programmes in India. This makes approaches like Child-to-Child difficult to integrate. It is important that child participation is taken as an umbrella framework so that those who work with children understand the value and respect that the approach places upon children. CHETNA has continued promoting child participation in all its work and is recognised as a resource group of the International Child-to-Child network. Prof Hawes passed away in July 2014 but has left behind a legacy of inspiration to continue our efforts in working with and empowering children.

The BvLF from The Netherlands supported CHETNA till 2012. Dr Judith Evans and Liana Gertsch supported our work and our mission of working with children.

The contribution of The John D. and Catherine T. MacArthur Foundation to CHETNA's organisational growth cannot be understated. Poonam Muttreja, the Regional Director for Asia, has been instrumental in understanding CHETNA's needs and building our competencies through critical questioning.

Dr Usha Jumani, a well respected management consultant, is an extremely valuable mentor. Over the years, she has facilitated three retreats for the CHETNA team (in August 2005, January 2007 and in June 2015). She was instrumental in helping CHETNA develop strategic criteria for project selection and also facilitated an evaluation of the CHETNA, Rajasthan office in 2004-05. Usha is passionate about organisational development and has taken a keen interest in CHETNA's growth and development. Her frank and candid feedback and meaningful insights have helped the CHETNA team reflect and evolve a definition of empowerment, gain meaningful insights on slow and fast track development, and on other critical organisational issues. She designed the entire management module for the WAH! programme. The pedagogy she helped develop for the 'Live project' in urban and rural areas has proved to be highly effective.

CHETNA's work and that of UNFPA intersected on a number of occasions in the 1990s, and the decade thereafter. The parallel journeys continued, with both the organisations subsequently giving greater attention to emerging concerns, for example, reproductive health and rights of young people, and to challenges such as gender biased sex selection. Ena Singh of UNFPA recalls this association.

> Prior to the International Conference on Population and Development, which was to be held in Cairo in 1994, there was a great amount of discord between government and NGOs, amongst NGOs, and between donors and NGOs with regard to the way population programmes were being implemented. Major bones of contention were around the quality of care, the reliance on targets and incentives, and the fact that programmes were narrowly focused

on family planning rather than on a comprehensive package of reproductive health services which would better meet the needs of women. At that time, as part of a pre-ICPD consultative process, led by civil society and supported by Ford Foundation and UNFPA, a number of meetings were held around the country. Fourteen regional meetings and four thematic meetings provided the space to express and resolve many difference, and to find common ground. CHETNA was very active in this process, and in fact co-anchored the thematic meeting on reproductive health and rights. The common ground forged by civil society led to a constructive dialogue

Evidence Based Advocacy with Dr Prakasamma (Founder Director ANSWERS and Formerly WHO South Asia) and Dr Ravi Duggal (2005)

Making a point at a meeting on Young Peoples Reproductive and Sexual Health and Rights

with government, and a common stand being taken in Cairo. A strong contingent went from India, with many representatives from the NGOs that had been part of the consultative process, including CHETNA. The forward-looking views that India articulated at the Cairo conference contributed significantly to the path-breaking agreements reached at ICPD.

Back home from Cairo, the government decided to lift method-specific contraceptive targets in a few districts, and shortly thereafter across the country. Instead of population programmes, they decided to implement a nation-wide reproductive and child health programme. This new approach threw up challenges relating both to the technical content of service delivery within service institutions (for example, how would states and districts design public health protocols for health services going beyond family planning and maternal health to include, say, Reproductive Tract Infections (RTIs) and adolescent health), as well as programme management and design at the district level. UNFPA took up the challenge, committing to designing and funding district-specific reproductive health projects which could show the way both on technical issues as well as programme management and design issues. CHETNA was one of the NGOs that contributed to this conceptualisation and design in Rajasthan and Gujarat.

As UNFPA worked intensively in Gujarat for a few years, there were greater opportunities for collaboration and cross-learning. The state formulated a women's policy, with UNFPA facilitating the work of government in leading the process where civil society and expert views could be brought forward, articulated, debated and reflected in a rather forward-looking policy. Again, CHETNA and UNFPA were partners, sharing perspectives and jointly advocating for a vision of gender equality and women's rights.

Working with CHETNA was always an opportunity to learn and share. Their vision was always clear: to collaborate for change. In my many interactions with CHETNA, I noticed that Indu's leadership style was very different from the norm. She reposed a confidence in her team, a confidence that went well beyond words. It was never 'always Indu' that one would see at meetings. Other staff would represent CHETNA, whether it was at a brainstorming meeting, or a formulation exercise, and their depth of knowledge and insightful analysis always left one grateful for their contribution. This is only possible when the leader delegates in a real way, as Indu obviously did. At the same time, there is an ease in the air at CHETNA. Not quite a 'family', not quite an 'office'. Something magical that brings the two together in a way that makes for a very effective, and sustainable, organisation.

When CHETNA decided to focus its work on nutrition and health issues, we engaged and interacted with several community oriented doctors and learned tremendously from their insights and experience.

We spent substantial time in the rural hospital and training centre run by Dr Lata Desai and Dr Anil Desai, doctors from SEWA Rural, Jhagadia in Bharuch district. Dr Ashwin Patel, Dr Anil and Dr Daxa Patel were working in Mangrol in Narmada district. These doctors had left their practices in the US and returned to serve the displaced communities due to the building of the Narmada dam. We spent a week at their field sites along the banks of the Narmada, learning about preventive and social health issues which were critical in health education. Not only were these doctors experienced/experts in community health issues but they were also very scholarly and suggested books for us to read, including Karl Marx and other social reformers. This gave our health communication efforts a solid base.

CHETNA's longest partnership with a doctor has been with Dr Samir Narayan Chaudhuri, the co-founder of Child in Need Institute (CINI) located on the outskirts of Kolkata in 24 Parganas. I had read about CINI and about its founder, a paediatrician from All India Institute of Medical Sciences (AIIMS), New Delhi, who had dedicated his life to treating children and mothers with severe malnutrition in remote areas of

West Bengal. Dr Samir Narayan Chaudhuri is really committed to the cause and what I really admire about him is his down to earth attitude and simple living. It is inspiring to follow him around and watch him counsel mothers with malnourished children, hear them call him 'Doctor Babu' with such reverence. When we realised that malnutrition and ill health in children is closely linked to poverty, low status of women and denial of rights to women and children, both CHETNA and CINI adopted a participatory strategy, working with village and local self-help groups, mostly of women and later including adolescents. Recently I had an opportunity to visit CINI again after a long period. Samir has expressed his desire to step down and he seems to be slowly withdrawing from day-to-day project management issues. One sees other senior members taking charge of different departments. I have learnt and I hope to continue learning from him and his organisation.

"I was charmed in the early eighties when I met Indu with her lively team of women colleagues from Gujarat at various national and international conferences and seminars mostly in Delhi and other parts of the country," recalls Dr Samir Narayan Chaudhuri. "As the conference organisers were arranging the venue, hours before the inauguration, Indu and her colleagues would trail them with suitcase loads of CHETNA publications, till they got what they wanted – a prominent display site! I would often relate this to my colleagues at CINI, and urge them to follow the persistence of their CHETNA colleagues to promote publications. The simplicity of their messages and the attractiveness of CHETNA publications make them very effective in transmitting complex information on nutrition, child and women's health."

The long term partnerships that have nurtured CHETNA, the mentoring we have received from representatives of some funding agencies and the perspectives we have learnt from other like-minded individuals have remained with us far beyond any project funding cycle. CHETNA remains indebted to all of them.

15

The troika sustaining the organisation

Coming together is the beginning
Keeping together is progress
Working together is success
— Henry Ford

At almost every forum where I am invited to talk about the 'success' of CHETNA, I am invariably asked one question: how did the three founding members of CHETNA meet and what is the magic recipe for staying and working together for more than 30 years?

Meeting Pallavi and Minaxi at VASCSC was a coincidence. Working together was a choice motivated by shared passions, dreams and aspirations. There have been many ups and downs over the past three decades, but our collective dream and vision has served as the glue that keeps us working together.

I met Minaxi Shukla, chemistry major, when she was volunteering on the Integrated Nutrition and Health Action Programme (INHAP) I was working on in VASCSC. She enjoyed working with children. I travelled for 20 days every month in the villages, and every time I returned from the field, Minaxi would patiently listen to my stories of how the supplementary food was not reaching the young children and how the nutrition information being imparted by us was making little difference in their lives. She was very interested in what I was doing. In support of my cause, she volunteered to translate the education and information material on nutrition developed by me into Gujarati, a language with which I was not very conversant. As we spent time together, I learnt the nuances of the local language and she picked up 'nutrition knowledge'.

In 1981, the INHAP needed additional staff when the scope of the project increased from 10 villages to 100 villages. Minaxi was interested in joining but since she was not a nutritionist, she was not selected. Pallavi Naik applied for the post and was selected. When we needed to expand our team further, Minaxi formally joined the project in 1982.

I was obsessed with developing strategies and worked tirelessly to find solutions to improve the health and nutrition of women and children. The three of us would sit around a table and brainstorm on how we could bring about this change. In the beginning, our dreams and aspirations for the marginalised were coloured by our urban lives, but continued exposure to rural areas broadened our perspectives. We began aligning our aspirations with their realities. We became convinced that education, particularly creating awareness among the marginalised, and in particular women, would change their status quo. We soon realised this would mean we would have to be patient to see results because women cannot and do not take independent decisions on their own; they are socialised into consulting family members and constantly seek approval from them and the wider community.

In 1984, when I was asked to write a concept note by Ford Foundation, I wrote about our collective dream and we gave it a name – Centre for Health Education, Training and Nutrition Awareness, or CHETNA. The sanctioning of the proposal was a great surprise and it definitely meant a long term commitment to our dream of creating an equitable society where women and children are valued and their nutrition and health concerns are addressed.

I do not remember the exact moment when we decided to work together. For me, CHETNA was not going to be a job to be completed between 9.00 am and 5.00 pm. It was going to be the realisation of my passion for improving the lives of marginalised women and children. My sense of responsibility and belief in participatory decision-making meant that I acknowledged and included the aspirations of Minaxi and Pallavi. I strongly believe that unless people take ownership of tasks/actions, it is impossible to achieve a collective vision. I was a nutritionist by training. It was but natural that I would be interested in issues of health. For Minaxi, who was always extremely fond of children and education, her career goal was to contribute to an industry related to textile chemistry. For Pallavi, who was looking for an outlet for her creative pursuits, getting involved in designing education materials was exciting. For Minaxi, who had studied Master's in Organic Chemistry, specialising in dyes, her volunteering work in VASCSC as a student had changed her perception in life. She realised investing her energies in education the children was her calling.

Though we are of the same age group, optimistic and enthusiastic, we have different skill sets, which complement each other and which have helped us in working towards our mission and building CHETNA. We operate collectively using our individual skills and competencies to forward our common goal. We have pursued our personal journeys alongside achieving CHETNA's mission. Pallavi has a passionate interest in developing graphic illustrative material. She had applied for a fine-arts diploma but eventually chose to complete her Master's in Nutrition. CHETNA has given her an enabling environment to express her creativity and satisfies what she liked doing most i.e. designing materials. Minaxi, who is passionate about children's issues, is a great asset in crafting popular messages and slogans, especially in the local language.

As we worked, I realised that all three of us needed to hone our competencies and skills through exposure to academic study of what we were doing intuitively in the field. So when I received an invitation to attend a workshop on participatory training approaches to nutrition and health led by Dr Lyra Srinivasan at National Institute of Public Co-operation and Child Development (NIPCCD), New Delhi, I requested NIPPCD to accept all three of us.

Minaxi and Pallavi were travelling to Delhi for the first time. Their families were concerned about accommodation, as NIPCCD did not have a hostel. I convinced their families that I would look after them. We stayed together in a flat of a friend of mine nearby the NIPPCD office. Our learning's from the workshop were invaluable for the kind of educational approaches that CHETNA has developed over the years.

This was closely followed by a Training of Trainers conducted by Participatory Research in Asia (PRIA).

Learning together: Training on Participa-tory Methodology at National Institute of Public Cooperation and Child Development (NIPCCD), Delhi (1984)

Minaxi and Pallavi, on completing the training, encouraged by their positive experience, requested all other senior colleagues also be sent for the training.

There are major differences in our skills and experience and at no point have I tried to impose my viewpoint on them, but rather we try to convince each other of our respective perspectives on an issue. Decisions are taken by consensus most of the time, and I feel that this participatory and inclusive management style has played a critical role in keeping their motivation alive. That is not to say this collective functioning has not had setbacks. It has affected the integration and motivation of the younger members who joined the team later. As it was practically impossible for all newly-recruited team members to work directly with me, I organised their responsibilities, based on their passion and interest, to report to Pallavi or Minaxi.

As expected, both of them have different managerial styles. Minaxi works with compassion and emphasises process. Pallavi operates in a participatory management style which encourages autonomy and independence while focusing on results. Individual team members learnt and thrived.

As the organisation grew and projects multiplied, I felt a need to review and evaluate our impact, and review our competencies as we were trying to excel in an environment which now demanded measurable outcomes. Mere good intentions were not enough. We commissioned an evaluation by PRIA which defined for us the direction we needed to take to make better impact.

Due to our varied competencies and comfort zones, we slowly started taking on different roles. I realised that policy advocacy was both my skill and passion. Working on the ground we faced a lot of barriers due to faulty policies. My desire to share and disseminate our learning's in order to influence policy took me to the national sphere, and internationally, since I realised that a country's nutrition and health policies are greatly influenced by agendas set in the West. An example is the universal acceptance of institutional delivery in India as a solution to high maternal mortality figures. This is an unrealistic policy for a country like India, where home deliveries are nearly 10 to 60 per cent (particularly in marginalised populations) and our health institutions are not yet ready to receive the load

CHAPTER 15

The troika sustaining the organisation

The Troika in 2000

of deliveries nor are doctors agreeable to staying in remote corners of the country.

As the challenges and expectations from the external environment grew (a number of developmental organisations had mushroomed all over the country, leading to more competition for the limited funds available), I once again realised a need to build the competencies of the senior team. For this, I approached, Pragati Leadership Institute from Pune to conduct a 360 degree feedback of the entire team. This was followed by personal counselling of all the leaders and training on team building, time management and leadership skills.

Since CHETNA's work was gaining credibility both nationally and overseas, my time away from Ahmedabad increased tremendously. I shared information with all and CHETNA undertook consultancies and assignments according to expertise and interest. Increasingly I felt that the load and benefit of the consultancy work should be more equally shared by all specially the senior team members. All my colleagues are now well known in their own area of expertise and many of them have also branched off as freelance consultants.

Still together for over 35 years (2015)

Pallavi, Minaxi and I revisited the organisation chart. We were clear that we prefer a participatory, decentralised and a lean organisation where everyone is a leader in their own right and they are enabled to function autonomously and take decisions in their area of work. The approaches and processes are based on non-negotiable principles. Gender sensitivity, valuing traditional knowledge, participatory decision-making, and people-centred approach are at the core of our organisation. By adhering to this, we have focused on our work and approaches, but it has also meant refusing some very attractive assignments which may have helped in fund-raising. I believe as NGOs we need to base our work on values. This may affect the organisation's funds in the short term but will result in keeping credibility intact.

The troika, as we are often called, use our complementary sets of skills to sustain the organisation. We have built acceptance and respect for each other, allowed each other space and autonomy to develop and continue to remain true to our shared vision. This has held CHETNA in good stead for over three decades.

16

Leadership transition

> I have admired the slow but admirable transition that has taken place in CHETNA over the years as Indu has made way for the younger generation to take over, a rare phenomenon in organisations founded by charismatic leaders.
>
> — Dr Samir Narayan Chaudhary, Secretary and Founder Director, Child In Need Institute (CINI), Kolkata.

I was first acquainted with Rashidah Abdullah, the co-founder of Asia-Pacific Resource & Research Centre for Women (ARROW), when she was working with the Asia Pacific Development Centre (APDC) in Kuala Lumpur, Malaysia. Rashidah and her colleague Rita Raj were compiling a book on women's health resources in the Asia Pacific when they came across the women's

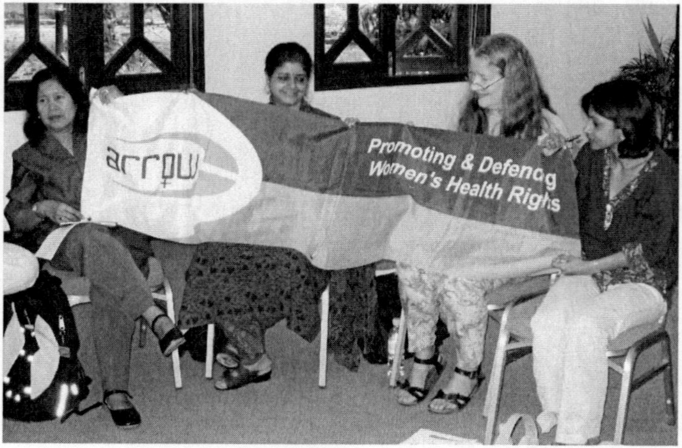

Sisterhood at the international level for promoting and defending women's health and rights

health kits developed by CHETNA. Impressed with our work, she wrote to me asking about the process that went into developing these kits. She featured CHETNA's kits in the APDC healthcare resource book.

When Rita Raj and Rashidah co-founded their own organisation, ARROW, in Malaysia, they invited me to a workshop on developing a gender sensitive health kit. That was our first meeting. Rashidah has a remarkable intellectual understanding of participatory research, particularly on women's issues. I, on the other hand, have hands-on experience of building an effective women's organisation. Our respective skills complement each other and we get along like a house on fire.

As Rita resigned from her managing role, Rashidah became a sole Director and she decided to expand the Board of Directors. Di Surgey, from Australia who had served two terms on Programme Advisory Committee (PAC) of ARROW was invited to serve. Rashidah entrusted the governance to carefully selected, skilled board members. Apart from Di Surgey, she selected me

A working lunch at a Board Meeting with Soul Sisters Mailyn from WHO and Dr Di Surgey from Australia

from India along with Zainah Anwar from Malaysia as members of the ARROW board. Though I was the youngest, I had experience of building a woman's organisation from scratch.

Rashidah, being an insightful researcher, researched how board meetings should be conducted and structured the ARROW board meetings extremely well. The meetings were exhaustive, held over two days, often in beautiful locations in Malaysia. They were extremely participatory, where every board member would chair one session and prepare for it. A lot of preparation and research is necessary to make a board meeting productive. Rashidah always listened carefully to each member's viewpoints and then would guide us to reach a balanced decision.

Rashidah also had clear criteria for whom to select and how to select board members. She was very clear that the board would consist only of women members working on women's empowerment. The women she chose to sit on the ARROW board were either those who had started and managed an organisation for at least 10 years, or were gender researchers who had the experience of writing/publishing gender related publications. All board members were evaluated at the end of their term on the board and their term renewed based on their performance, not influence. Terms were limited to two. The ARROW board developed organisational tools and policies after consideration of examples drafted or introduced by the Executive Director, staff or individual board members. Many of these tools and policies are still being used in ARROW.

The ARROW board meetings I attended were the most enriching phase of my life. Governance in CHETNA was developed from my learning's at the extensive brainstorming sessions as part of ARROW's board meetings. I not only learnt how to conduct effective board meetings from Rashidah, I credit her for inspiring me to plan leadership succession and handing over the reins of CHETNA.

Rashidah had been toying with the idea of stepping down for a while. She felt ARROW needed new, youthful leadership. She gave the board six months' notice. She drew up a shortlist from her acquaintances and professional colleagues, including me. I declined her generous offer as I did not want to shift base to Malaysia. When she couldn't find anyone suitable from the shortlist she had drawn up, she placed an advertisement. As usual, Rashidah had done extensive research on the selection criteria. She wanted ARROW's leader to have extensive knowledge of the development sector and the women's movement, have strong documentation skills and experience with strategic planning and organisational building. She rejected most applications she received. In the last week of her notice period, she received one that she found promising and invited me to join her in conducting the interview.

A consultant had drafted the core competencies required by the Executive Director of ARROW with input from the Board. This was used to shortlist the candidates and I was invited to be part of the interview panel. We conducted the formal interview in the veranda of Rashidah's home (as she was unwell) and chose Saira Shamim (Sham) to succeed Rashidah and lead ARROW.

•

The experience of observing the professional way in which Rashidah managed change in ARROW's leadership got me thinking about the same at CHETNA. This was in 2009. I discussed my tentative plans with several peers at various conferences I attended. They were all surprised, as was the senior management and governing council at CHETNA. Our long-term funding partners also expressed concern about the change. Everyone felt I should delay my decision. But I knew CHETNA needed a new leader. However, it took me a long time to act on my decision.

I finally began actively searching for a successor in 2010. Being a value-based organisation, we hesitated to post an advertisement. As news of my decision to step down spread, I started receiving feelers from several senior government officials. I met several possible candidates from both compassionate NGOs and community based organisations that CHETNA had trained and from professional managers, even from the corporate world.

I believe there are three skills a leader of any organisation requires in today's world: ability to understand and work with latest technology, be comfortable with data and numbers as markers of achievement, and have the ability to build relationships and raise the visibility of the organisation. CHETNA's future leader, I was sure, must have all of these as well as in-depth knowledge of the social issues we work with, strong oral and written skills to document and communicate our work and a participatory approach to help sustain our vision and mission. CHETNA's gender sensitive systems and processes have evolved over time. I was keen these be continued and supported further. Where I continuously faced a dilemma was choosing between a young outsider with state-of-the-art IT and management skills or a loyal insider who understood our work, had internalised CHETNA's vision and mission, and would more easily support existing systems because they had been involved in developing them. My experiences in building capacities of women leaders have shown that generally women are hesitant in taking on leadership roles. In contrast, men, particularly those from a management background, actively pursue leadership opportunities. While I had not pre-determined that my successor had to be a woman (unlike Rashidah and ARROW), it is my belief that majority of men in senior management positions tend to be a stickler for systems and less empathetic to concerns of employees, women in particular. This, I felt, would not be suitable for a woman-centric organisation such as CHETNA. But I wanted to keep an open mind.

When I communicated the decision of stepping down to my governing council I was advised that we may choose an internal person as my successor. We conducted a 360° evaluation of the entire senior management team at CHETNA. The governing council short-listed Pallavi and Minaxi as the best candidates to take CHETNA forward. It was a difficult choice as all three of us had worked together since the inception of CHETNA. Pallavi is extremely creative, an independent thinker, balanced and diplomatic. Pallavi has also contributed significantly in making CHETNA visible in the virtual space and had developed CHETNA's website. Minaxi has wonderful people skills and is cautious in her approach, listening and understanding all sides before taking a decision. Both had always been reluctant to take on any administrative responsibilities in the running of the organisation. It was a testing time for me. I had to put all personal considerations aside and make a choice. After much inner turmoil, I recommended to the Board that Pallavi would be the ideal candidate to take the baton ahead.

My conversation with Minaxi informing her of the governing council choice was far more difficult for me. Minaxi, on the other hand, did not seem surprised. "It was clear to me from the very beginning that I was never going to be your choice to take over your post," she told me. "Whenever you were away from office for long periods on tour, you somehow designed

With Pallavi Patel (Director, CHETNA since May 2013) (1990)

the responsibilities in such a way that Pallavi was left in-charge. This was a clear indication of your future choice." But when the decision was formally announced by the CHETNA governing council, Minaxi, being an emotional person, reacted adversely.

When I spoke with Pallavi, she was initially hesitant. She asked why the council had chosen someone from inside CHETNA. I told her of my reservations of bringing in an outsider who may not be able to understand and preserve CHETNA's ethos and culture. She said, "Indu, I will manage the internal co-ordination, but you continue

Celebrating with the CHETNA Team (1991)

to manage external relations and negotiations with government agencies, funding agencies, etc." I spent a lot of time, across several conversations, convincing her that division of the responsibility of managing the organisation was not desirable. However, if she was absolutely unwilling to take on the role, then I would have to look for someone from outside. Pallavi, like me, did not prefer this option.

Mentally Pallavi was waiting for her children to settle down before she committed to the leadership role. She was particularly hesitant to travel to Delhi to advocate with the national government. To get her used to the idea of leadership, she first took independent charge of all projects related to women and young people, including their financial management, while I continued to travel and meet funding agencies. She slowly started taking independent decisions and began to feel more confident.

Initially, Minaxi found it very difficult to be accountable to Pallavi as she was used to reporting to me. The main reason was our difference in leadership style. On the other hand, Pallavi who was trying to establish her authority; would get frustrated as Minaxi would rarely go to her for direction. In addition, Minaxi had been given the designation of Additional Director (till then, they both had the same designation of Deputy Director), which led Pallavi to expect that Minaxi would take over some additional responsibilities. As role clarity between the two was not formalised, it took a lot of time to resolve the conflict that arose. My availability and presence in the transition has proved to be a blessing in disguise as Pallavi could discuss issues with me when there was a difference of opinion between her and Minaxi.

Often people ask me why Minaxi did not resign when she was not chosen to lead the organisation. I myself have asked her this question. "Indu, working for children through CHETNA gives me immense satisfaction. So, even though I was disappointed by your decision, I no longer think of it, because I continue to do the work which satisfies me." What has been her experience in CHETNA? I asked her.

> For me, the journey with children began even before CHETNA was born. I visited VASCSC in 1967 on an exposure visit organised by my school. Inspired by the philosophy and child-centred environment and

activities, I continued my association with the Centre. Having enjoyed the joyful learning experience as a child, I volunteered at the Centre all through my school and college years and joined VASCSC formally as a research associate for the project on environment awareness through community education. The project included developing and implementing environment education approaches and activities with school children in Gujarat. Later, I joined the INHAP project.

While I enjoyed working at VASCSC, I chose to obtain a Master's degree in organic chemistry, specialising in dyes, with an aspiration to establish a production/processing unit compatible with the textile industry in Ahmedabad, which was the textile hub of the country. However, my interest in working with children and disadvantaged communities got ignited into passion after Indu joined VASCSC in 1980.

Impressed by Indu's personality, I started interacting with her, volunteering to translate nutrition and health messages and materials. Through our interactions, I started learning about nutrition and health from a community health and development perspective. After formally initiating CHETNA as an organisation in 1984, the learning process has continued, not only for me but for everyone who has joined CHETNA at different stages of our evolution and development as a unique resource organisation in the field of nutrition, health, education and development of children, women and young people. In the first decade of working at CHETNA we were exposed to numerous challenges; we travelled to Uttar Pradesh, Rajasthan, Bihar and Odisha to conduct training programmes; we worked with teachers and community health workers field testing our learning resource material. CHETNA is not merely an organisation; it is a dynamic phenomena, always evolving.

CHETNA has always believed in its people, that it's the team which is the organisation. While Pallavi and I have been two legs of the tripod, Indu has been the strongest leg. Our backbone is our diverse competencies, which complement each other. Indu is a tough task master and yet an extremely tender-hearted human being and a friend. She identifies and nurtures the potential and passion in a person and provides appropriate opportunities and challenges to work, prove and progress. This motivates those who work in CHETNA to give their best to the work and the organisation. Indu always thinks holistically, whether it is for CHETNA as an organisation or on the issues of children, women and young people's development, and yet always guides the team to remain focused. She represents and promotes CHETNA wherever she goes.

I am an introvert and shy. But Indu inspires and always brings out one's hidden qualities and confidence. This has helped me to reach out, express my views and ideas at local, national and international forums when representing CHETNA and also as a child advocate. My passion for working with children found a strong platform and a niche in CHETNA.

I have never looked back and have never regretted not pursuing a career based on my educational qualifications. I have also realised that having passion is necessary when working with social issues; yet it is equally important to manage your passion strategically and systematically to achieve your mission. Organisational management and structure is also vital. CHETNA has taught me this inevitable truth.

Pallavi has gained Minaxi's respect and has proved over time that she is the right choice. Pallavi has taken over all the responsibilities, learning new IT skills, financial management skills and, most importantly the skills of being accountable to herself and others. She is consultative and open to taking feedback and suggestions on her decisions. I am confident that she will steer CHETNA towards a sustainable future. Her experience at CHETNA has been somewhat similar to Minaxi's, she tells me.

> I completed my MSc in Nutrition from M.S. University, Baroda. I shifted to Ahmedabad since my parents stayed there. The city was new to me. I was unaware of work opportunities, but took the lead to meet people and apply for jobs. I luckily received two opportunities — one in SEWA and the other at VASCSC. I opted for VASCSC for two reasons — one was the short commute from my home to office; the other was the presence of Indu Capoor who was my senior during my post graduation.
>
> During my Master's, I had got an opportunity to work at the community level. That exposure was extremely enriching and I wanted to continue working in this direction. CHETNA gave me that opportunity. I learnt the realities of disadvantaged communities through my work at CHETNA.
>
> CHETNA, especially Indu, put tremendous faith in me and provided me several opportunities to grow and get exposure. This created a strong foundation for my continuation in CHETNA. Attending the ToT in Participatory Learning Methodology at PRIA

helped me contextualise what we were doing through CHETNA.

I also had an unspoken desire to work in a creative field, and given the freedom at CHETNA to design and develop health communication material, which I still enjoy. I enjoy simplifying information and presenting it for a community to learn from. In the initial years, when I was involved in the child survival programme, I got an opportunity to work with SEWA and Sadguru Water and Development Foundation (SWDF). Training health workers at SEWA and women workers in SWDF is one of the richest experiences of my work here. Working with underprivileged communities and women's empowerment in CHETNA has also given me courage to take a stand to bring about change in my personal life.

On several occasions Indu and I have had differences of opinion and viewpoints, but we derive strength from each other by sharing the differences to amicably reach appropriate solutions. We may not have always agree but we respect each other's views, and many times we agree to disagree.

•

Change is never easy, and this change in leadership at CHETNA was not without tension. Many staff started feeling insecure when they heard I was stepping down. At the same time, funding agencies were demanding greater 'accountability' from CHETNA with respect to 'evidence', and we needed to set up accountability and M&E systems. First, we had to institute time plan sheets. A near rebellion broke out in the organisation as in the NGO sector people are not used to accounting for the time they spend on people-centred processes. Funding agencies are unable to accept this, as they want to see outputs and outcomes as the result of the time spent by programme staff. Being a firm believer in professional integrity, we agreed to the introduction of time sheets as a tool to streamline processes. Analysis of the Time Plan Sheets (TPS) revealed several inefficiencies. This did lead to some staff attrition. Every project now has an M&E system in place to assess the output/outcome of the project.

Another demand from funding agencies was documentation, both qualitative as well as quantitative. While programme teams at CHETNA were comfortable writing qualitative/descriptive reports, it was difficult for them to write up quantitative indicators. Programme staff had to develop the skill of objective analysis and writing. It was no longer an 'option' but a necessary skill for every CHETNA team member to have. Senior team members reflected on their own documentation skills and slowly realised that loyalty and extensive field experience alone were no longer going to be enough to contribute to CHETNA's future growth.

As I slowly became free from the administrative and managerial responsibilities of running an organisation, I decided to use the time to visually document CHETNA's journey. When CHETNA completed 30 years in 2014, we mounted an exhibition of CHETNA's milestones.[2] Photographs were dug up from archives and interviews with team members led to trips down memory lane. It also created a sense of belonging and ownership within the organisation.

I continue to be a mentor, going in to the office only when Pallavi needs my support in undertaking

---

2. See *http://www.mediafire.com/download/gayceycyvfh2ezm/30_years_Penal.rar*

a specific task she has not done before, for example, preparing for the board meeting. I now have more time for advocacy and conversations to bring changes in health and nutrition policies for women and children. And yes, I wrote this book.

SECTION

FOUR

Re-visioning Organisations

17

Recognising gender sensitive organisations

I really felt good in my heart on my first day at CHETNA when the administration department asked what I would prefer as the prefix to be used with my name. This made me feel comfortable and accepted in the organisation immediately. Till date, I have never been treated differently from others. CHETNA has provided me with an enabling platform to think beyond my limitations while simultaneously mainstreaming people like me who are part of a sexual minority community [transgender and third gender].

— Mr Kartik Gore, training officer at CHETNA

The first thing that people remark when they visit CHETNA is that it is a gender sensitive organisation. How can they perceive this? It is because our work culture, organisational structure, and values, the governing council, selection processes, the physical space we sit in and even our logo reflects gender sensitivity. We have ensured that gender is integrated into our vision, mission, goals, objectives, management and decision-making. CHETNA has a mandate and commitment for gender equality. An organisation that is not gender sensitive cannot bring about change in the public and private space where women and men live their lives.

We did not begin with an organisational theory of creating a gender sensitive organisation. We learnt it by doing, through trial and error. In spite of our sensitivity to aspects of gender, both in our work and in our structures and processes, we too had blind spots. Pallavi, Minaxi and I were all raised in primarily gender neutral families. Yet, when we began creating illustrations for our manuals and Information Communication Technology (ICT) material, we did not create gender neutral messages/illustrations. We drew from the realities of the field, and often created pictures without giving a thought to whether they were discriminatory towards women and girls. For example,

With Board Members of ARROW Malaysia Di Surgey, Rashidah Abdullah (Founder Director, ARROW) Marina Mahathir and Rashidah Shuib

ARROW
BOARD OF DIRECTORS

we placed men on *charpais* and women sitting on the floor as it existed in the rural communities in which we carried out our work. We corrected this as we learnt that patriarchy in Indian families also influences the food habits and health seeking behaviour of women, young people and children.

It was much later in 2005 when we realised the logo we had created for our organisation promoted a gender stereotype. CHETNA's initial symbol was an image of a mother and child. This clearly depicted who we work for and in fact was very appreciated by the community based organisations we worked with. But one day it was brought to our attention that through the symbol we were re-enforcing the social reality that a child is the sole responsibility of a woman alone, while the gender equal practice which we were promoting both outside and inside the organisation was that both parents need be responsible to look after the needs of a child. How had we been so blind?

At the time, CHETNA was beginning to work with young people and we realised that the logo of mother and child did not reflect this emerging area of our work. It also did not convey the life-cycle approach we adopted, of including men and boys in the health and development of women and children.

CHETNA's initial logo (1982-2005)

In our search for a new logo we held several consultations with our partners in the field and within the organisation. It took almost two years to come to a consensus. These inclusive and participatory processes are at the soul of CHETNA's work. We finally agreed on the current logo, as we felt it projects CHETNA's image as a gender sensitive organisation which works to remove gender stereotypes and strives to change the status quo.

When we introduced the changed logo, we

encountered resistance, particularly from NGOs and community based organisations working in the field. Interestingly, the explanation of the different elements of the logo has become a great talking point during trainings to introduce the topic of gender among communities. It has also become a vehicle to explain CHETNA's vision and the perspective of a gender balanced society.

CHETNA
For Women Young people Children

The current logo symbolises many aspects of gender and life, integrating eastern and western logic of individual rights with social responsibility for balance and harmony.

Through centuries, patriarchal forces have restricted the spaces for women and controlled their mobility through fear, shame and silence, creating stereotypes and disempowering women. These spaces and norms are a dividing line between men and women, often referred to as *dahleez* (threshold) in north India. The symbol illustrates the awakening of consciousness and self-awareness of women, young people and children to challenge the *dahleez*.

The inner and outer circles represent the awakening of dormant energy, translating into dynamic energy in the future. The inner circle represents consciousness and self-awareness emanating from self-motivation. It draws reference from the widely known Tao symbol of Yin-Yang representing balance and harmony of polar energies, constantly in motion, whose cyclic fluctuations and interactions cause and govern Creation. It also represents the womb. The outer circle represents dynamic energy. It is a continuation from the inner foetal form representing female energy.

The nine rays, representing the solar system, symbolise stability with change. The number 9 is the incubation period for the human foetus to reach its full term. Society/patriarchy has centred women's physical and emotional health during the nine months of pregnancy.

The spiral is a symbol of continuity, evolution, devolution, involution, expansion, contraction, cycles, mysteries and changes which are the natural result of all that has gone before. Here it represents the inherent energy of the dot (or atom); when released, it spirals outward, merging, converging with the dark, purple energy.

The spiral also symbolises the shell of a snail, the house which it carries around on its back. It is a metaphorical reference to the status of women under patriarchy. As lunar and solar symbols, snails symbolise death and rebirth. Being linked to the cycles of the sun and the moon, the snail became a fertility symbol in many cultures. Its shell was likened to a womb. Its horns and its slimy body were symbols of both male and female sex organs and conception. Here, combined with the form of the spiral, it symbolises emerging from the confined 'inside' to converge with the 'outside', crossing the *dahleez* to create a more complete world.

•

As a gender sensitive organisation, there are many gendered practices and processes in CHETNA which have been institutionalised. First and foremost CHETNA's governing council has a gender balance of both women and men. The first governing council chair was an eminent educationist, a woman. We now have an extremely gender sensitive man as the chair. All governing council members are carefully selected not only on the basis of their relevant expertise and experience but also on the basis of their gender sensitive beliefs and practice in everyday life.

All leadership positions in CHETNA are anchored by women. We believe that while competence and qualifications should not be compromised, qualities of compassion, collaboration and caring are critical to performing effectively as a leader. CHETNA also focuses on addressing women's practical needs and supports women to define and meet their strategic needs. In majority of its projects, efforts are made to mainstream gender equity and projects are regularly monitored to ensure specific needs of women, young people and children are being addressed through project interventions.

CHETNA's work culture and clear articulation of its values is an important part of the gender sensitivity of the organisation. Many organisations do not articulate their values clearly. Our experience has shown that there tends to be a gendered gap between the actions of staff in envisioning the values of the organisation. While women generally value relationships, men give undue emphasis to evidence and numbers. The values a gender sensitive organisation expresses should be conscious of these differences and acknowledge and accommodate the needs of both men and women.

Creating a gender sensitive organisation does not mean that women have to occupy all positions in the organisation. It should have men and women at all levels, with equal benefits. In 2015, CHETNA had a 50:50 ratio between men and women, including one transgender employee. The key ingredient in a gender sensitive organisation is empathy and fair treatment of all employees. A gender sensitive organisation recognises, enables, utilises and appreciates the talent and competence of every team member. But while the organisation cares and provides an enabling environment for all its employees to grow and develop, being gender sensitive could mean creating a bias in favour of girls and women. Development organisations working in and with communities have an added responsibility of transforming gender relations in society by incorporating empowerment of women into all their work, by valuing their productive and reproductive labour, and reducing the oppressive patriarchy within homes and communities.

In the new development paradigm there is undue focus on measuring outcomes and deliverables. Social change processes however need considerable time to be spent understanding the needs of communities, particularly of women who need more time to articulate their views. Policy makers and bureaucrats are often in a hurry to expedite completion of plans, and do not give space for such engagement. There is also a comfort level among policy makers (who are generally men) to consult their male friends. As a result, women's views, perspectives and experiences are left out in the planning process itself. Most men are ready to travel to the National Capital Delhi for consultations and meetings at short notice; women on the other hand cannot simply pack their bags and leave. If we are working for women, gender sensitive development organisations must advocate for development projects to be patient, to help women get ready to be able to voice their opinions in the language that they are comfortable with.

Gender sensitive development organisations working with women and child health need to advocate for policies that focus on nutrition, particularly of children and young girls. Giving additional food to communities who are suffering from the effects of water and air pollution can only have limited affect. In addition to food security, we need safe water, sanitation, nutritious and diverse food crops (agriculture), rich soil nutrition and, above all, pollution free environments. We need an agricultural policy which promotes food diversity and does not focus on cash crops alone. We need potable safe water and sanitation in order to reduce 80 per cent of preventable diseases which affect the health of women and children.

Increasing livelihood opportunities without studying the effects on children and women's nutrition and health status is not gender sensitive. Recently CHETNA conducted a study on the effects of increasing livelihoods through agricultural improvement and found very little difference among the control and intervention areas mainly because the development organisation undertaking the project did not feel it necessary to accompany their agricultural intervention with nutrition and health counselling among the families. At the end of the day, no amount of extra food will improve the nutritional status of adult women, particularly when they are overburdened with work. It is also a well known fact that when people come out of poverty they may not accept positive health behaviours automatically. For instance, poor families have started feeding their children noodles and biscuits, which are aggressively marketed. When families of low birth-weight babies start coming out of poverty and begin feeding their children, it is more likely that in later life these children will suffer from non-communicable disease like hypertension and diabetes.

The government system expects women to take on voluntary roles, for example, the ASHA in the health care system, or the teaching assistant in the education

Interactive dialogue in a gender course for young psychologists at Jyoti Sangh (2016)

sector, or the women who manage self-help groups. Most women take on this work not for the money but for the identity which it gives her. However, this should not be a way to exploit a woman's labour. Initiatives that promote women's work often pay less or impose additional responsibilities simply because policy makers believe that a woman's family has enough income and the income women earn is 'additional'. A gender sensitive development organisation must always be aware of such hidden assumptions.

Women's empowerment is a fashionable term these days but to ensure this in a developing country like India is quite a challenge. Women by nature are creators and they bring this quality to all that they do. They are also generally quite aesthetic as they observe and respond to nature and natural surroundings. People generally plan for both men and women as though they are same. In rural and urban slum areas, all women work round the clock to make ends meet and to fulfil their productive and reproductive roles. Sometimes, well-meaning livelihood programmes can add to her already 'overburdened' life. Our experience has shown that as women take on more responsibility, men shirk further from productive work. Gender sensitive organisations must change the mindsets of women and men if we are going to build gender equal societies.

Women by nature are nurturing and would like to lead 'wholesome lives' which include caring for families and leading a fulfilling work life. Presently, this seems impossible in our patriarchal structure. Look at the successful women leaders around. They all either have 'family support' (which could mean they are from elite family backgrounds) or they are single women. An average woman in India, living within limited resources, finds it extremely stressful to lead a wholesome life. She is expected to earn money and continue to fulfil the social expectations of her family, do all the household work, and take care of the children and elderly. This makes it difficult for her to take on leadership roles.

The media propagates messages which reinforce gender stereotypes. Planners are only thinking of economic growth with undue emphasis on livelihoods programmes, which may not automatically improve the health and wellbeing of disadvantaged families and communities. Resource allocation to the education and health sector over many budgets has reduced.

Our system conspires to produce robots. Men bow to family and peer pressure and work in traditional jobs that pay well and are well regarded by society, often ignoring what their inner voice may tell them to do. And women do the same, in addition to taking on

all household responsibilities. To gain respect and be successful in male dominated workplaces, they slowly acquire characteristics which define male leaders. And no one is really happy.

We need caring, compassionate and committed men and women at every level in all organisations. We need emphatic leaders, both men and women, who take decisions that promote inclusive, sustainable, gender equal development, particularly for the disadvantaged and marginalised sections of our society. We need men and women to build gender sensitive organisations and gender equal societies together.